Motoring on Regional Byways

WEST COUNTRY

Books for Motorists

Motoring on English Byways
Motoring on Scottish Byways
Motoring on Irish Byways
Motoring on Welsh Byways
Motoring Holidays in Britain
The BP Book of Festivals
Companion to English Highways
Companion to Scottish Highways

Books for Young People

Exploring the Countryside
Exploring the Rocks
Looking at Buildings

General Books

Greater London: Its Growth and Development Through 2,000 Years
The Cities of London and Westminster
The Changing Face of England
The Story of England in Brick and Stone
The Russell Family: Earls and Dukes of Bedford
Dictionary of Archaeology
Ireland (Collins Guide Book Series)
London (Collins Guide Book Series)
The Weather and You
Colour Photography
A-Z of Photography

CHRISTOPHER TRENT

Motoring on Regional Byways

WEST COUNTRY

Byway motoring in Somerset,
Gloucestershire, Herefordshire, Worcester-
shire and parts of Shropshire and
Wiltshire, illustrated with 32
photographs by the author

LONDON

G. T. FOULIS & CO. LTD

1—5 PORTPOOL LANE

E.C.1

First impression March 1968

© Rupert Crew Ltd 1968

SBN 85429 080 X

MADE AND PRINTED IN GREAT BRITAIN BY
MORRISON AND GIBB LIMITED, LONDON AND EDINBURGH

CONTENTS

ILLUSTRATIONS

vii

CHAPTER ONE

WEST COUNTRY BYWAYS

THE WEST COUNTRY has been variously defined, and on the face of it its boundaries are rather more vague than in the case of other accepted divisions of the country. For the purposes of the tours in this book the area covered comprises roughly the counties of Somerset, Gloucestershire, Herefordshire and Worcestershire, and in addition north-east Wiltshire and south-east Shropshire where these two counties project into their neighbours. So our motoring territory in the west stretches from the Devon border to the north Midlands.

There are, however, characteristics which are common to these far-flung districts. One of the highlights is the Cotswold, that extensive rolling plateau which reaches a height of over 1,000 ft in places, but the whole of the West Country is diversified by pleasant green hills, a great number of them wooded, none reaching 2,000 ft though the Clee Hills of Shropshire are only just under 1,800 ft and Dunkery Beacon on Exmoor rises to 1,707 ft. The Malvern Hills, extinct volcanoes on the Hereford-shire-Worcestershire border, because they rise abruptly from the plain to a height of nearly 1,400 ft give the impression of being a mountain range. But it is not until the Welsh boundary is crossed that the mountains become high and rugged ranges. On one tour we penetrate a little way into the Black Mountains across the border for a brief experience of mountain byway motoring.

All the above-mentioned hills and many others are explored in the course of the tours, for almost without exception there are roads around the slopes and numerous roads actually cross the summits, so that the rides are marked by magnificent views from high points. Yet because the West Country can be summed up as a land of pleasant green hills, its scenery is by no means tame and it is not without dramatic features. The most widely known is the unique and awesome Cheddar Gorge and its marvellous caves of stalactites and stalagmites, which have been made easily accessible to the public by skilled excavation and tasteful lighting.

Also in the limestone Mendip Hills is the scarcely less impressive Burrington Combe with its 'Rock of Ages', while the beautiful wooded Avon Gorge, spanned by the graceful Clifton suspension bridge, reaches to the very heart of Bristol. To the extreme west there is the grand cliff scenery of the north Somerset coast where Exmoor rises sheer from the sea and attains a few miles inland its highest elevation at the bare summit of Dunkery Beacon.

The mighty river of the west, the Severn, and its many tributaries, among which are the Wye, the Avon and the Teme, water a large part of the area we cover. They have dramatic highlights in many beautiful reaches and we shall drive beside their banks where possible in order to enjoy some of these.

Man's handiwork has contributed another typical feature of the West Country—its wealth of distinguished towns and villages in two contrasting building materials, each with its own characteristic style and each lovely in its own way. On the one hand there are the mellow Cotswold stone towns and villages, some of them almost too well known but many more lying off the beaten track just as picturesque and worth visiting as their more famous neighbours. On the other hand there are the beautiful timber-framed and half-timbered black and white houses of Worcestershire and the Marcher counties, a great number of them embellished with ornamental timber work in intricate patterns and richly carved. Numerous homes and castles in both architectural styles are open for us to visit and admire for their beauty as well as their historic interest.

The west since prehistoric times has been the haunt of man in retreat from superseding tribes from the east, as the rich legacy of prehistoric monuments and hill forts or camps testifies. At the coming of the Romans many of these sites were taken over and developed and we shall find many links with that period too. The Saxon heritage is less obvious, for they were people of the plains and valleys of the rivers and their settlements have become modern centres of population. Most of the many churches founded by the Saxons have been swept away and replaced by later buildings, but it is interesting to note that the beautiful cathedrals of Gloucester, Hereford and Worcester, to mention only three examples, were originally founded in the seventh or the eighth century. Many of the abbeys, too, were founded in Saxon times and then refounded in medieval times, and there are splendid abbey ruins to be seen, such as Glastonbury and Cleeve. Some of the beautiful abbey churches fortunately became parish churches, e.g. Bath, Sherborne and Tewkesbury, and are preserved in all their splendour to the present day. An interesting aspect of the Norman churches of the west is the influence of the Celtic tradition, seen in the churches of Kilpeck and Eardisley, and in the remaining fragment of the medieval Shobdon church.

In the later Middle Ages when the wool boom was at its height most of the Cotswold churches were enlarged or rebuilt in the spacious Perpendicular Gothic style, such as Chipping Campden, Cirencester and Northleach, a striking feature common to all being the magnificent tower. The 'Somerset' towers are outstandingly rich and lavish, with their intricate tracery, pierced parapets and pinnacles, for Somerset's prosperity was also founded on the woollen cloth industry. We shall find numberless examples of these beautiful soaring structures.

Somerset's plain makes up in historic interest what it may lack in scenic contrast. Glastonbury is regarded not only as the cradle of British Christianity but also as the Avalon of the legendary King Arthur, who fought a rearguard action against the encroaching pagans after the withdrawal of the Romans. Camelot, his fortified capital, is believed to be Cadbury Castle, which is now being excavated and has already yielded important finds.

King Alfred waged his famous campaign against the Danes in the marshes, culminating in the victory of Ethandun and the Treaty of Wedmore, and consequent baptism of Guthrum, the Danish leader, as a Christian at Aller. The last battles fought in this watery plain took place during the rebellion of the unfortunate Duke of Monmouth against his uncle, King James II. This was put down without mercy and hundreds of Monmouth's adherents were condemned to death by the notorious Judge Jeffreys.

If the boundaries of the West Country are indefinable, there is no doubt about its capital. Bristol is the acknowledged 'Queen of the West', a splendid city since it has risen again after the severe bombing of the second world war, centrally placed in the midst of grand country. The residents are, therefore, wonderfully well situated for touring in all directions from the city, which is easily left behind for the open fields. For the many visitors who make Bristol their centre there is plenty of accommodation of all grades.

Recently another gateway has opened for Bristolians with the completion of the Severn Bridge, giving swift access to Wales. I have not included any tours in Wales from Bristol using the Severn Bridge, as these do not properly belong to the West Country and in any case are already dealt with in my book *Motoring on Welsh Byways*. But the existence of the bridge underlines the command of motoring country enjoyed by Bristolians.

Bath is almost equally well situated and is another favourite base for touring, while for those who have a feeling for staying at the seaside, Weston-super-Mare is only 21 miles from Bristol, Clevedon only 13 miles. For the Cotswold and the Marcher counties more convenient centres are Gloucester, Cheltenham, Hereford and Worcester, as well as the many smaller towns in the vicinity. Farther west, for Exmoor and the north of Somerset there are Minehead and the smaller resorts along the coast, while inland there are the market towns of Somerset, from Taunton, the county town, to Yeovil near the Wiltshire border.

Happily there are no large industrial complexes to avoid in planning the tours, and the seemingly unlimited mileage of unspoilt byways makes motoring in this part of the country pure pleasure. Indeed it is scarcely ever necessary to take to the main roads, which themselves often have all the beauty of byways and prove almost as quiet. One might say 'Go West' still holds good as a slogan for the motorist in search of quiet charm.

CHAPTER TWO

SOUTH OF THE AVON

OUR FIRST TOURS explore the country south of Bristol, which, as we have noted, is singularly fortunate in its surrounding countryside as well as being a splendid centre for tours farther afield. If we have not previously visited the city, we must make an opportunity, preferably on a Sunday when it is quiet, to drive round its handsome modern centre, rebuilt after the bomb damage of the second world war, and to visit the surviving links with its ancient past.

Bristol has been an important port since Roman times, the port from which John Cabot and his son Sebastian sailed on their famous voyage to North America, the headquarters of the great Merchant Venturers of the Middle Ages, its traditions maintained by the handsome harbour and docks of the present day. Near the harbour and the river Avon are the two noble medieval churches, the cathedral and the parish church of St Mary Redcliffe. The cathedral dates from the twelfth century and parts of that early Norman church remain in the transepts and the chapter house. This church was almost entirely rebuilt in the fourteenth century, apart from the tower which was added in the fifteenth century, and this rebuilding survives as the nucleus of the present cathedral, although it has been enlarged to almost double its medieval size by later additions. The interior is spacious and impressive and contains many early monuments and tombs.

St Mary Redcliffe has the distinction of being described by Queen Elizabeth I as 'one of the goodliest parish churches in England' and few will disagree with this dictum. The great cruciform church is almost 240 ft in length and the west tower is crowned by a spire 292 ft high, soaring above the surrounding buildings. One of its most beautiful features is the Decorated hexagonal chapel which now forms the north porch, and inside

5

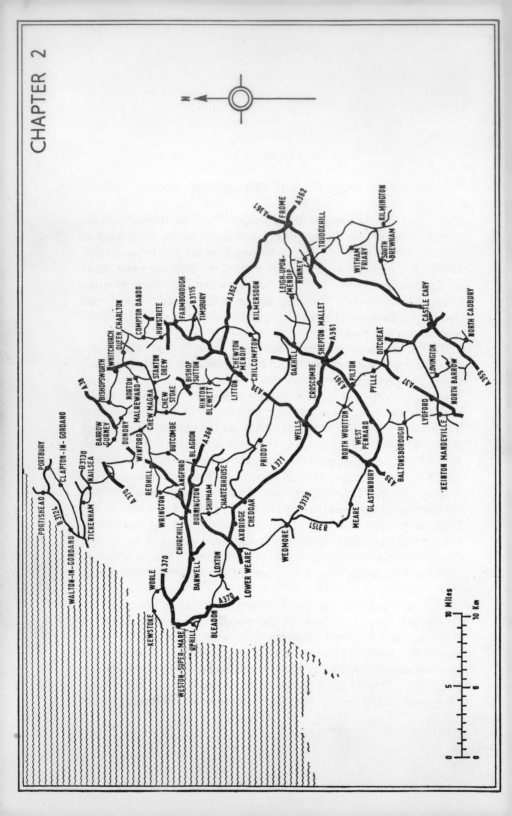

the church there are many ancient memorials. There are a number of other medieval churches, including the Mayor's Chapel in College Green, where we shall find also the Norman St Augustine's gateway, which has a later Gothic upper storey.

Coming down to more recent times, there are elegant Georgian squares and streets, as well as handsome individual houses, as we climb away from the harbour; the Cabot Tower on Brandon Hill in the midst of lovely gardens and the impressive modern buildings of Bristol University, of which the twentieth-century Gothic tower is a distinguished landmark.

There is plenty of accommodation in Bristol to suit all purses and requirements, especially in the residential area around Clifton Down, high above the main part of the city. This is a convenient centre for the tours in this chapter, as in each case (except for the Wells tour) we leave the city by the Clifton suspension bridge, Brunel's graceful masterpiece (although it was not completed until five years after his death in 1859).

The following tour of about 110 miles along the Bristol Channel and over the Mendip Hills to the world-famous Cheddar Gorge begins, therefore, by crossing the suspension bridge, thus obtaining fine views into the impressive limestone gorge with its densely wooded cliffs. Thence we go straight ahead and into Ashton Park, the beautiful wooded demesne of Ashton Court, built by Inigo Jones in 1634. We drive right through the park to the Clevedon road, B3128, in sight of Long Ashton's handsome church, and continue along this road for a mile or two, and in the midst of a strip of woodland on the right of the road we turn right for Portbury and Portishead along a pretty wooded road between the hills.

On reaching Portbury we turn left for Portishead, at the subsequent junction noting an old building, formerly part of an ancient priory, the rebuilt part now being used as a school. From Portbury to Portishead we are in Gordano, a triangular plain or wide valley bounded by two long ridges. In Portishead we can make a detour to the esplanade and beach, and encircle the headland of Portishead Point, at the farther end of which is a gigantic power station. The town and port are interesting, and in the old village, beside the church with its tall pinnacled tower, the ancient manor-house survives, retaining its Elizabethan turret. We leave by the road which passes the church (Church

Road South) and turn right into Slade Road, turning left uphill at the next crossroads and turning right short of the 'Bay' hotel, then left along the cliff road, a fine coast road running high above the sea for over three miles (we turn right at the T-junction to continue along the cliffs).

At Walton Down the cliff road turns inland and descends steeply to Walton-in-Gordano, where we turn right in B3124 and in about half a mile turn right for Walton St Mary, with a good view on our right of Walton Castle on top of the hill, an old house with four round towers at the angles of its outer wall. Our road shortly takes us into the pleasant resort of Clevedon, and we drive along its attractive promenade and past the pier and then up a cliff road to the farther promontory ending at Wain's Hill, which is crowned by a prehistoric hill fort (this is reached by a footpath beyond the old church). We must return from this grand viewpoint to the town and drive through it on the Bristol road, which passes Clevedon Court just beyond the town. This is a manor-house dating from the time of Edward II, with Tudor additions, open to the public on Wednesday, Thursday and Sunday afternoons from April to September, also on Bank Holiday Mondays. The entrance is beside the lodge on the left of the road.

From Clevedon Court we retrace our way as far as the end of the park wall and there turn right in All Saints Lane (marked unsuitable for heavy traffic) through the charming village of East Clevedon lying under the wooded hill called the Warren, past the modern Gothic church, and right on a major road beyond it. We bear right at the next junction for Clapton-in-Gordano, and when we leave the houses behind there are fine views over the whole of Gordano. We follow this pretty road under one wooded ridge and looking across the valley to the other, then after more than three miles come to the ancient church, dating from the thirteenth century, and the fourteenth-century manor-house of Clapton Court, which has a turreted tower and Gothic windows. In the main part of Clapton village we turn right towards Portbury, and shortly right again in the road signposted Wraxall. This road climbs over the ridge, with fine retrospective views across Gordano, and at the summit crosses a bridle way to Cadbury Camp. There we go forward for Nailsea and turn right at a T-junction on a cliff on the other side of the ridge, looking across to the range of the Mendip Hills.

The towering lime-
stone cliffs of the
Cheddar Gorge,
Somerset.
(Chapter 2.)

The magnificent west
front of Wells
Cathedral.
(Chapter 2.)

Nunney Castle and
its surrounding moat.
(Chapter 2.)

Vicar's Close, Wells,
claimed to be the
oldest street in Europe.
(Chapter 2.)

We continue on this road into Tickenham, forking left to the church in Church Lane. Cadbury Camp is now on the hill to our right but the trees obscure the entrenchments. Tickenham church has the unusual dedication St Quiricus and St Julietta and an interesting tower with a statue in a niche on each parapet face. Here we bear left for Nailsea and on reaching it turn right towards the 'Butchers Arms' at the crossroads, then turn left beside it, going along Union Street and turning right into Church Lane. At a T-junction just beyond the typical church we turn right and follow this road to a signposted junction, where we turn left for West Town and soon pass the manorial group of Chelvey—the Jacobean Chelvey Court, now a farm, with several ancient barns, beside the partly Norman church.

At the next junctions Brockley and Brockley Combe are signposted and we drive through the high rocks and woods of the combe. After two miles we turn right opposite a letterbox and just before a telephone booth, skirting an aerodrome and then reaching the village of Redhill, where we bear right for Wrington. We continue to Wrington (page 58), turning left into the High Street, right at the post office, and leaving on the Bridgwater road past the church. We continue on this road to Langford post office, where we turn right, again for Bridgwater, in half a mile going forward in A38. On the summit of a hill to the left of us are the vast earthworks of Dolbury Camp and after going through Churchill, the home of the Duke of Marlborough's ancestors, our road runs through a gorge under Dolbury Hill. We bear left at the top of the pass for Rowberrow and then go forward for Cheddar through Shipham village, turning left on A371 as we descend towards Cheddar. In the village we turn left on B3135, rather oddly signposted 'Cliffs', which takes us through the Cheddar Gorge, unique and deservedly famous. Few fail to be impressed by the sight of these awe-inspiring cliffs rising sheer on either side of the road. The caves, with their beautiful stalactite and stalagmite formations, should not be missed by anyone who has not previously seen them.

We avoid the turnings to Bath and Bristol, continuing on B3135 over a grassy plateau and going forward at all crossroads (Chewton Mendip and various other places are signposted). This road keeps up on the high plateau with extensive views in all directions. Care is needed when crossing A39 and the next

road, B3139, soon after which we turn right for Croscombe at a
crossroads, then in less than half a mile left over a railway,
thereafter following the signposts to Frome, largely on the course
of the old Drove Road on a high ridge all the way.

Frome is one of the most interesting of Somerset's many
market towns, as it retains one or two of its narrow streets almost
unaltered and looking as they must have done in medieval times.
Cheap Street, in particular, is a narrow market street lined with
timber houses, their overhanging storeys reaching out towards
each other across the street, and a little stream or gutter running
down the centre. The medieval church is an exceptionally fine
one and combines all styles from the Norman to the sixteenth
century, and is remarkable for its several side chapels. The
restored market cross stands in the centre of the wide main street,
formerly the market place, and at the top of the hill the Congrega-
tional church of 1707 is a handsome building in the classical
Queen Anne style.

We leave Frome by the Radstock road, then take the middle of
three roads, signposted Mells. We reach this beautiful village in
just over two miles, with its groups of mellow stone cottages,
some thatched, building up to the dominant church, which has a
richly decorated Somerset tower. Beside it is a splendid Elizabethan gabled manor-house. We drive through the village on
the Radstock road and follow this road as far as Kilmersdon,
into which we turn, going under a railway bridge, after following
the park boundary of Ammerdown House. (The grounds and
gardens are occasionally open to the public during the summer
months.) Retrospectively we can see the memorial column on the
wooded hill in the park.

At the end of the village we go straight on and soon after
passing a classical entrance arch beside a lodge we turn right at a
subsequent junction for Shepton Mallet, later crossing A367, the
Foss Way, for Wells, but immediately turn right up an avenue
marked by a stone pillar, crossing a subsequent major road
beyond the other end of the park, where there are two stone
pillars at the entrance. From here we descend into the village of
Chilcompton, crossing a railway on the outskirts and turning
right as we enter the centre. We continue on this road and go
straight on through the pleasant neat houses of a mining com-
munity and at the 'Oakhill House' inn turn right for Timsbury.

We continue to Timsbury, forking right after crossing the green track of a disused railway at an unsignposted turning, and right at a T-junction at a wider road, descending into a little combe and finally climbing up to the hillside village of Timsbury, passing several Georgian houses. There are good views to our right across the Cam Brook valley before we turn left by the 'New Inn' just beyond the church.

We shortly cross a major road for Farmborough, where we turn left by an inn on reaching the village, going through the pleasant centre with houses beside a rivulet running along the main street. One fine old house on the left bears the date 1667. When we reach the main road we turn sharp right, but at the top of the hill turn left for Hunstrete. At the next junction we bear left, then shortly right, which brings us in less than a quarter of a mile to a major road where Compton Dando is signposted. We follow this, in another quarter of a mile forking right downhill along a pretty winding lane which takes us through the hamlet of Hunstrete to the quaintly named village of Compton Dando. Here we bear left by the medieval church and war memorial cross for Chewton Keynsham, crossing a pretty reach of the river Chew, and almost immediately turning left again up a steep narrow lane between high banks, bearing right at a fork in sight of a modern house.

When we reach the summit of this road we have a wonderful view across the Chew valley as well as in all other directions. At a crossing road on the plateau we turn right past the Queen Charlton concrete works, and then go forward in a wider road towards Queen Charlton, steering towards its church tower and soon forking left to reach it in a little link lane, and left again at the village outskirts. In the attractive centre the old village cross on high steps stands on the village green opposite St Margaret's Church, which has a Norman tower. Opposite the west end of the church we shall find a fine Norman doorway used as a garden entrance. This was originally the gateway of the abbey court house.

We continue past the church on the Whitchurch road and on reaching a major road we go forward to a main road, in which we turn right into Whitchurch and at the church, in about a quarter of a mile, turn left for Bishopsworth. We follow this road to Bishopsworth, thence returning to Clifton and Bristol.

The next tour, which is a shorter one of approximately 70 miles, continues our exploration of the Mendip Hills and takes us to the old town of Shepton Mallet and the fascinating prehistoric monuments of Stanton Drew. Again we leave Bristol by Clifton Down and the suspension bridge, bearing right at the other side of the bridge, then right on A369, signposted Clevedon, then left, again for Clevedon, and in a mile and a quarter left for Providence. We have thus half encircled Ashton Park. Now we turn away from the park, crossing a major road, our way again signposted Providence, and descend a steep hill. This takes us through Providence and at a subsequent main road we turn right and follow it briefly, after half a mile turning left in the road signposted Barrow Hospital. This is a narrow lane which brings us in a mile and a half, just beyond some pine trees, to another main road by the shore of a reservoir, where we turn right into Barrow Gurney. Before we reach the main part of the village, however, we turn sharp left uphill in a narrow lane just beyond a group of farm buildings. (If we wish to see the village, quite a pretty one, we shall find one or two Tudor and seventeenth-century buildings, and the Elizabethan Barrow Court near the church, which is to the west of the village and over a mile from it.)

We cross the main road, A38, half a mile from Barrow Gurney, and near the crossing have a good view along the reservoirs of the Bristol waterworks. Now we continue to Winford, there forking half right at the 'Prince of Waterloo' inn for Winford Manor. When we reach the estate wall of Winford Manor we go over the crossroads righthanded, neglect two subsequent left turns, passing a small wood soon after the second one, and take the third one, signposted Blagdon. Our road now proceeds towards the main ridge of the Mendips, which dominates the skyline ahead as we descend into Wrington Vale, driving through the pretty little village of Butcombe clustered in the combe of a tiny stream, and we pass its post office on our way to Blagdon. Soon our road runs beside the west end of the vast Blagdon Lake and when we leave the lake we go forward immediately into Blagdon, distinguished by the tall tower of its church. In Blagdon's main road we turn left for Bath, but in about 100 yards fork right for Charterhouse. As we climb up the hill out of Blagdon there is a superb retrospective view to the lake and the village, and there is a fine parking place on the left.

Beyond this the road climbs higher and higher, giving a glimpse of the Chew Valley Lake to our left, and at a fork on the hill we take the left branch. At a subsequent T-junction on the summit we bear left towards Cheddar, but soon leave this wider road for a turning on the right to Charterhouse. This village, now only a small hamlet, has an interesting history. It takes its name from a small Carthusian foundation but all signs of this have long since disappeared. The district has, however, links of much greater antiquity, for it was an important Roman lead-mining centre. The amphitheatre for the entertainment of the miners is still to be found on the hill above Charterhouse up a grassy lane to the west of the Blagdon road. Many interesting finds from this Roman period have been made in the slag heaps near the mines. The highest point in the Mendips, Black Down (1,067 ft) is just over a mile to the north-west of Charterhouse.

From the village we continue to Priddy, noting that the landscape is still pitted with old lead workings, on the way to Priddy crossing a B road (with care) and later another B road right-handed. In Priddy we go straight on at the village cross-roads, leaving the church across the fields to our left. This village with its large central green is on the high plateau of the Mendips and it, too, was an important mining centre dating back to Roman times.

The road continues over the plateau after leaving the village, crossing a crossroads after about a mile and a quarter, then reaching A39 in another mile and a half. We turn right in the main road, then in half a mile left opposite the entrance to Penhill Farm. This road follows the edge of the plateau and we have grand views across Sedge Moor to Glastonbury Tor. We turn left in the next major road for about a quarter of a mile, then right just short of a large inn. In another half mile we turn left at a wider road, which we follow over a railway, where it is signposted Croscombe, and shortly turn right for Croscombe. This road takes us into the village in the valley in just under two miles, and we turn right into it. The spired church is reached by the lane beside the old village cross, and is worth seeing for the ornate Jacobean wood carving inside, and there are several ancient houses in the village.

We turn left opposite the 'George' inn, going over a bridge and bearing left at a chapel steeply uphill, turning right at the first junction, then left at a subsequent T-junction, and so into Shepton Mallet, turning left into it on the Frome road, then across the traffic lights for the market place and church. Shepton Mallet is famous for its exceptionally beautiful stone market cross, which dates from the fifteenth century. It is an open hexagonal structure with a pierced parapet and pinnacles, and rising from its centre is an elaborate spire in three stages with Gothic arches and pinnacles. The nearby church has a good Somerset tower and inside a magnificent timber panelled nave roof.

We leave Shepton Mallet by the High Street, downhill from the market cross, at the end of the town going under a lofty railway viaduct, 200 yards beyond which we fork left into an unsignposted lane. We continue on this lane, now in the stone wall country of the Mendips, and neglect turnings to the left until we come to a T-junction by a Georgian farmhouse, where we turn left along a currently unsurfaced road, crossing a major road at the summit of the hill and descend on the other side, now on a surfaced road, to a main road at the foot of the hill. We turn left in this road, A37, passing the 'Mendip' inn, and half a mile beyond it fork left into an unsignposted road by a stone-built farmhouse towards the far-seen tower of Binegar church, which our road later passes. Soon afterwards we cross a sign-posted crossroads towards Wells but at the next T-junction turn away from Wells and bear right for Bath, leaving this road, too, in a quarter of a mile and forking left on an unsignposted road. We keep straight on in this road, crossing a track, and later a wider road, as we go over a ridge, driving between stone walls and hedges, in a landscape with scattered trees amd long views as we descend gradually.

At the next crossroads we go forward for Chewton Mendip, the splendid church tower of which beckons us. In the attractive village centre we cross the main road for Litton, to which we continue on this road, B3114, going through a little hamlet of cottages beside a stream. Litton is another charming village and we fork left on reaching it to see the old 'King's Arms' inn and mill house, then right into the village centre at the next junction to make an almost complete circuit of the village, but just before reaching our original left turn we bear left by a group of new houses. We fork left again in a few yards for Hinton Blewett, right at the next T-junction, and fork right again shortly up, a hedged and banked lane which brings us to the hilltop village of Hinton Blewett grouped round its towered church. There are grand views south from the village centre, where we turn right for Bishop Sutton and go on towards it along another pretty hedged lane over the breezy plateau.

At the village of Bishop Sutton we cross a main road for Chew Magna, passing a placid reservoir set under the hill to our left. We neglect various side turnings on our way to Chew Magna, ascending through bracken-covered commons under Knowle Hill, and just beyond the hill turn left in a wider road and reach Chew Magna by its old mill and mill house on the river Chew. This once important little town has some well-preserved old houses in the main street, which has a raised causeway. The spacious church, with typical tower, has some interesting tombs and monuments, and at the churchyard entrance the medieval manorial court building survives. The old manor-house of Chew Court is also near the church.

Before continuing on our way from Chew Magna we must make a detour to the neighbouring village of Chew Stoke, following the signposted way and noting the seventeenth-century manor-house to the left about halfway between the two places. Chew Stoke is one of the most picturesque villages in the county, with a tributary of the river Chew flowing through the centre, which we cross into the village, then recross it beside an ancient stone bridge of two arches to reach the church, which has an elegant tower with a spirelet. In the lane leading to the church is the early sixteenth-century rectory, which has many heraldic shields on the wall.

We return to Chew Magna and resume our way towards Bristol on B3130 but by a hexagonal thatched house, formerly a toll house, we turn off for Stanton Drew. On the way to the field containing the famous prehistoric stone circles we pass near the bridge a medieval rectory with Gothic windows opposite a later manor-house. The entrance to the field is beyond the church and admission for a fee of threepence can be obtained at any time on weekdays. The monument consists of three stone circles and is thought to be of the same date as Avebury. There are also the remains of two avenues leading from the two larger circles, and in the garden of the 'Druid's Arms' is a prehistoric burial chamber, known as the Cove, which can also be viewed on any weekday at a fee of threepence.

We return from Stanton Drew to the toll house and turn right in the major road, then left beyond a garage up a lane prohibited to heavy traffic. We keep right at the first fork and drive through Norton Malreward village, which lies under Maes Knoll, its summit crowned by the extensive entrenchments of a prehistoric camp. At a T-junction beyond the church we turn left for Dundry, thereafter following the signposts to Dundry. To our left the Chew Valley Lake comes into view as we climb higher and higher to the village. The views are even more remarkable from the village centre (almost 800 ft high) across the whole Avon valley. The tower of Dundry church was built in the mid-sixteenth century by the Merchant Venturers. It is tall and graceful with a richly ornamented parapet, and can be seen for many miles. Outside the church there is part of an old churchyard cross and a large 'dole' table.

We bear right past the church, going downhill and bearing left into the village street along a shelf road, looking down on the Bristol reservoirs, then we bear right downhill and so back into Bristol.

The next tour is routed from Wells, because although it is only a small cathedral city many come to stay at its ancient hostelries in order to explore its unique medieval heritage and they may well wish to know something of the surrounding countryside. But first something must be said about Wells, which in its central position in the county is within easy reach of Bristol, Bath, Glastonbury, Wincanton, Frome and also from the seaside towns from Portishead to Burnham. Motorists from these and other places have plenty of time in one day to see Wells and then follow the tour. From Wells back to Wells the distance is roughly 55 miles.

The wells from which the city takes its name are seven deep springs which feed the moat of the Bishop's Palace and supplied the city with water from medieval times onwards. Near these springs the first church was built at the beginning of the eighth century by King Ina of Wessex, and two centuries later it became a cathedral. In common with most Saxon churches, it was rebuilt in the twelfth century but in this case the style used was one of the early essays in the Early English Gothic with pointed arches.

The glorious west front is also in the Early English style and was completed in 1239. The wonderful screen of statuary is a fascinating study, with its several hundred ecclesiastical and royal figures, spanning the impressive width of this west front flanked by the dignified towers. One of the most intriguing features is the ancient astronomical clock with its brave procession of knights on horseback as it strikes the hours. This is inside the north transept, and on the outside clock-jacks strike the quarter hours.

Near the lovely chapter house and the north porch is another unique link with the Middle Ages. This is the Vicars' Close, connected with the church by a covered way over the Chain Gate spanning the road. This street of stone houses, each with its tall chimney, was built for a college of singing clerks, or vicars, in the mid-fourteenth century and although modernized still gives an impression of medieval domestic architecture. The close is claimed to be the oldest street in Europe. At the far end is a picturesque little chapel, while the common dining hall is over the entrance gateway.

The Bishop's Palace is on the south side of the cathedral beyond the cloisters and a drawbridge over the moat leads to the imposing gatehouse. The palace buildings are within the enclosure and are still the residence of the Bishop of Bath and Wells, only the great hall being in ruins. The view to the palace across the moat from the lawns, usually with several swans sailing along majestically, the swans which traditionally ring a bell for their food, is a memorable one and it would be difficult to find a more beautiful place. Near the broad walk on the west of the moat the stone building with many buttresses is the ancient granary of the bishops.

Added to this feast of ecclesiastical beauty, there are many other medieval buildings in the town, the various gateways of the cathedral close, including 'Penniless Porch' leading into the market place, several ancient inns, and the quaint almshouses of Bishop Bubwith in Chamberlain Street.

Reluctantly we must drag ourselves from this trip into the Middle Ages and return to the present. We leave the centre by the Shepton Mallet road but in a mile, at a well and fountain at Dulcote, we turn right for North Wootton, then left round a steep hill, later bearing right over a railway at the approach to

Dulcote quarry. Thence we continue to North Wootton and West Pennard, the road following a long low ridge along its foot, then along A361 for the last two miles into West Pennard.

We continue on A361 towards Glastonbury, but two and a half miles short of the town turn left for Baltonsborough, where at the crossroads by a war memorial we go forward for Barton St David, our road running beside the canalized river Brue and lined here and there by graceful willows. Soon after crossing the canal we turn left at a junction where Keinton Mandeville is signposted, there turning left on B3153 towards Castle Cary. We cross the Foss Way at Lydford, and at the next village, Lovington, turn right for North Barrow, following the signposts into the latter. We go through the village with the church on our right and cross the railway just beyond a junction, then continue to a main road, A359. Here we turn right for Sparkford but in just over half a mile left for North Cadbury, steering towards a line of attractive, partly wooded hills.

North Cadbury has an exceptionally good fifteenth-century church built for a college of eight priests, and added to an earlier tower, while Cadbury Court beside the church is a splendid Elizabethan manor-house with typical gables. These both lie off the village street, to which we must return and turn right for Woolston, going forward into a narrow lane, a 'hollow way' between high banks.

When we come to a wider road we turn left for Yarlington, but where the Yarlington road turns left we go forward for Wincanton and straight on again at the next two junctions, our way now signposted Shepton Montague, but at the next junction our way is signposted Bruton. At the next crossroads we turn right for South Brewham, then left, going under a railway, then bearing right on to a ridge road, at South Brewham turning right for Kilmington. There at the summit of the hill on which Kilmington stands we turn squarely left on the way signposted Witham Friary, down a wooded and rhododendron-lined hill with an immense view forward over the Frome valley.

At a junction at the foot of the hill we go straight on for Frome and Trudoxhill, this road taking us through Witham Friary village. One of the few Carthusian monasteries in England was established here and the present church was attached to this foundation. All the conventual buildings have disappeared but an interesting survival is the monks' dovecot opposite the church, now a reading room, which gives an idea of its exceptional size.

We continue past the church for Trudoxhill and there turn left through the village towards Nunney, crossing a subsequent main road just before reaching this outstandingly picturesque village, happily grouped beside its ruined castle. Nunney Castle, which was built in 1373, gives the impression of a complete building from across its surrounding moat because the walls of the massive rectangle with four round angle towers are almost intact. The building is in the care of the Ministry of Works and can be viewed daily (admission fee sixpence). The church with a lofty tower lies on the other side of the Nunney brook, and there is a very pretty corner looking across the brook to the church from the castle. The handsome manor-house in the Wren style, now a farm, is also near the castle, while there are some ancient stone houses in the village.

We leave Nunney by the Mells road, but leave it in a quarter of a mile, forking left into an unsignposted lane, subsequently bearing left and passing the Asham quarries by a stream, then ascend steeply up the opposite hillside, and shortly at 'Ye Olde White Horse' inn turn left in a wider road for Shepton Mallet. We continue towards Shepton Mallet until Leigh-on-Mendip is signposted, where we turn right then go over the crossroads and soon see on our right across the fields the noble tower of Leigh church high above the houses clustered round it. In the village we bear left for Oakhill, and in Stoke Lane (Stoke St Michael) we cross the village street right-handed by the 'Knatchbull Arms' and go on to Oakhill, which lies on A367. Here we turn left and although we are soon almost 900 ft up our road gives no real indication of its height. Soon after joining A37 we turn right at a crossroads for Wells, going over the crest of the Mendips, and we can now see that we are on a high ridge, with views on each side, over the Somerset Plain to Glastonbury Tor and the Quantocks on the left, and towards the Avon valley on the right. This fine road takes us back into Wells in just over five miles.

The final tour in this chapter is routed from Weston-super-Mare (quickly reached from Bristol via A370). The distance from Weston back to Weston is rather under 90 miles. This former fishing village on the Bristol Channel has become a flourishing and popular seaside resort visited by many thousands every year. Its broad promenade backed by hotels and shops runs along Weston Bay for over two miles, looking to Worle Hill, crowned by the prehistoric Worlebury Camp, on the north and Brean Down on the south. We begin the tour by driving south along the promenade to its end at the car park on the sands, then turn slightly inland to drive almost parallel with the sea for a further short distance, at a junction going straight on for Uphill. Near the end of Uphill village we go forward for Highbridge, shortly crossing a main road for Bleadon Hill, over which we climb, enjoying long views across the marshes to Brent Knoll behind Burnham-on-Sea. We descend to Bleadon village, where we turn left, leaving the church on our right, thence follow a course between Bleadon Hill on our left and the river Axe on our right. We pass the handsome manor-house of Loxton on a high point to our left as we approach Loxton, and from there our road is along a southern shelf of the range, so that we are still looking out over the marshes.

We are now making for Axbridge and are soon driving along its High Street past the old manor-house of the early seventeenth century, which is open to visitors on Wednesday afternoons from the beginning of May until the end of September. The High Street leads to the spacious central square, in which there are several ancient gabled houses with overhanging upper storeys, notably one on the corner known as King John's Hunting Lodge. The splendid church of St John the Baptist stands in a dominant position above the north side of the square.

We return from the market place to the main road, following the signposts to Bridgwater as far as Lower Weare, where we turn left for Wedmore and continue on this minor road all the way to Wedmore (about four miles). On reaching Wedmore (page 63) we turn left on the Wells road and after passing the church turn right at the next T-junction, and right again in 100 yards, signposted Glastonbury. We are now driving over the marshes with their raised roads and many willows lining the drains. In Meare just beyond the church we pass the quaint Abbot's Fish House, built 1335, and the nearby manor-house of the Abbot of Glastonbury.

We proceed towards Glastonbury, driving for some distance beside the canalized river Brue, then shortly entering the town (page 45). We drive to the abbey, then continue on A361 for

Shepton Mallet, passing under the slopes of Glastonbury Tor, the tower on its summit clearly visible. We drive for another two miles on A361 as far as West Pennard, where we turn right for West Bradley. In sight of the church to our left we bear right past a fine stone mansion with typical Jacobean gables, then soon afterwards, just after a sharp left-hand bend, we turn right by a poplar tree, finding a short distance along this road the ancient Court Barn (National Trust), a magnificent stone building with buttresses. At the next signposted junction we bear left for West Bradley, right at the next junction for Baltonsborough, then left for East Pennard, going forward for the latter where another road joins ours, then almost immediately right for Lydford, right again for Lydford, then continue straight on for Castle Cary, following the signposts into the centre of the town.

Near Castle Cary's mellow market house and later town hall above, we turn up Bailey Hill to see the old circular stone lock-up by the Georgian post office in the square. It is dated 1779 and is one of the only four surviving in the country. Fore Street leads from the market hall to the site of the castle from which the town takes its name, and the picturesque Horse Pond with its graceful swans and the island war memorial mirrored in its waters. There are many old houses and inns in the town and All Saints church in the Perpendicular style is a spacious and distinguished structure with a pinnacled tower and tall spire. We leave by the Wincanton road, fork left for Ansford, and at the top of the hill turn left for Shepton Mallet on A371, which soon crosses the railway, and at 'Brook House' inn turn left for Ditcheat. We reach Ditcheat by its impressive church, where we turn left and then immediately right for Glastonbury. The church, which has a central tower, has a fine angel roof and a carved wooden pulpit and reading desk dating from the reign of Charles I. The old rectory north of the church dates from the fifteenth century.

At the next T-junction we turn right, away from Glastonbury, and bear left at a subsequent junction, and left again in a short distance at a fork signposted East Pennard. Half a mile farther we come to our old friend, the Foss Way, otherwise A37, in which we turn right towards Shepton Mallet, looking towards the Mendips. When we reach one of the few villages on the Foss Way, Street on the Fosse, we turn left for Pylle Manor and

Pilton. We pass the Elizabethan manor-house of Pylle opposite the church, and a charming roadside lake and go on to Pilton.

Pilton is a most attractive composition, with an impressive church in a commanding position on our right, and the manor-house, contrary to the usual tradition, on a hill rising above the church. To the left of our road there is an ancient gabled tithe barn, now roofless, which formerly belonged to the Abbots of Glastonbury. Beyond the church we continue for North Wootton, shortly crossing A361, and in North Wootton go on to Wells (page 16), leaving that city by A39 for Bath, but at the end of the built-up area by a belt of trees turn left on the Old Bristol Road, bearing right at a junction. We are soon in the heart of lovely Mendip country, gradually climbing to the summit among limestone cliffs and outcrops of naked rock, where the walls are also of the limestone.

We continue straight on, going over several crossroads and passing the 'Castle of Comfort' inn, a well-known landmark on the summit, where our road, now B3134, bears left for Burrington. A little over four miles from the inn we begin the descent into Burrington Combe, an impressive gorge with steep limestone cliffs and fine rock formations, broken up with many fissures and faults. A deep cleft from top to bottom of the cliff on the right gave shelter from a storm in 1762 to the Rev. A. M. Toplady, who thereby composed the hymn 'Rock of Ages'.

At the end of the combe we enter the village of Burrington and after passing the church turn left in A368 towards Weston, crossing A38 at Churchill and going on to Banwell. We drive through Banwell with the church on our right and leave by West Street, but near the end of the village fork right for Worle. We drive over the marshes to Worle, keeping left at a T-junction where Kewstoke is signposted, shortly crossing A370. We continue to Kewstoke from Worle, and pass its ancient church (the steps known as Monk's Steps, opposite the church, lead to a magnificent viewpoint) as we take the toll road, a lovely wooded cliff road above the sands and sea, back to Weston.

CHAPTER THREE

THE VALE OF SEVERN

THE COUNTRY to the north of Bristol is just as rewarding as that to the south. The rich Vale of Severn stretches away to the north far beyond Gloucester and is bounded on the east by the outliers of the Cotswold Hills. That part of the vale in which the city of Gloucester lies is known as the Vale of Gloucester; the part below Gloucester and lying along the south bank of the Severn as the Vale of Berkeley, dominated by its ancient and historic castle. In the foothills to the south of Gloucester we shall find picturesque old market towns which grew up when Cotswold wool was famous all over Europe, and the tradition is carried on to this day in the clothmaking industry centred in this area.

The tours are equally suitable for motorists in Bath, which is also an ideal centre for holidaymakers and has ample accommodation of all kinds. Bath achieved more than ordinary fame twice in its long history, first as the great Roman town of Aquae Sulis which grew up around the hot springs, then as the fashionable spa of the eighteenth century centred on these same springs. The ruins of the Roman baths, which were thoroughly excavated towards the end of last century, give some idea of the first town's magnificent public buildings and temples. The baths can be visited on every weekday and on Sunday afternoons, and there is an interesting museum adjoining them where a model of the original baths can be seen and also many objects dating from the Roman occupation which have been found in the vicinity. It is perhaps not surprising that in both periods Bath developed as a place of entertainment and recreation as a result of the attraction of its healing waters for great numbers of visitors.

The unique Georgian city is happily there for us to see, a superb essay in the mellow Bath stone of the local quarries, built mainly by the Woods, father and son. There is nothing in England to equal compositions such as the Royal Crescent, the Circus

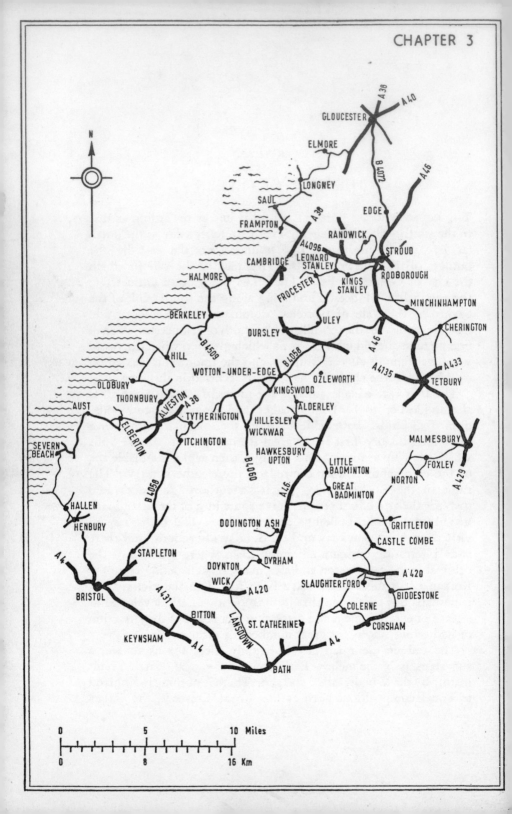

The Vale of Severn from Sanfords Knoll, near Frocester, the silver ribbon of the river on the horizon. (Chapter 3.)

Robert Adam's Pulteney Bridge in Georgian Bath. (Chapter 3.)

Valley of a tributary of the Avon near Tadwick.   (Chapter 3.)

Dursley's market house, with a statue of Queen Anne on the front of the upper storey.   (Chapter 3.)

and Queen Square, to quote only three examples. The Assembly Rooms and Prior Park were also built by the Woods, though the Pump Room was rebuilt late in the eighteenth century. Pulteney Bridge was also built late in the century, the only contribution of Robert Adam to the city, and a very graceful one with its charming rows of shops. It is easy to understand why Bath was visited by the famous and the fashionable during its heyday.

Bath's fame as a Roman and Georgian spa rather overshadows its medieval history but the fine abbey survives to underline the importance of the city in the Middle Ages. It began as a Norman cathedral which was destroyed by fire in the twelfth century while still incomplete. The abbey of today was founded at the beginning of the sixteenth century, a lofty and spacious building typical of the Perpendicular period with splendid fan vaulting. The enormous west window is flanked on the exterior by angels ascending and descending ladders, said to represent a dream of the founder, Bishop Oliver King. As might be expected of a city which so many of the great made their home, the abbey contains an unusually large number of monuments and memorial tablets.

Those are just a few of the fascinating aspects of Bath. There is so much to see that a day is not too long to spend in exploring its elegant crescents and squares, its grand public buildings.

The first tour, which takes us to one of England's prettiest villages, Castle Combe, the medieval town of Malmesbury, and several historic homes, is approximately 110 miles from either Bath or Bristol. If the start is from Bristol, we take the A4 towards Bath as far as Keynsham, if from Bath we take the A4 towards Bristol to the same point. There we turn left (right from Bath) for Bitton at the medieval towered church and soon cross the Avon by an ancient stone bridge and continue over the water meadows of the broad valley to Bitton, turning right to the village on A431 (an alternative point to join the route either from Bristol or Bath). In the village centre we turn left in Golden Valley Lane, now running alongside the bank of the river Boyd in a fertile green valley, passing several fine mills and mill houses.

We keep close to the river without crossing it, making for Beach, and when the road leaves the river go forward over the next crossroads into this little hamlet of the hills. Beyond it we fork left at a T-junction for Cold Ashton. We continue in the green hills, the distinctive Freezing Hill crowned by a prehistoric entrenchment imminent to our left. We go forward for Marsh-field at the next crossroads, then right towards Bath at a junction with a 'no through road', soon joining a wider road over a breezy ridge commanding a distant view of Bristol on the right and a deep valley to our left, towards which we take the first turning on the left just before reaching the race-course on Lansdown Hill.

We descend to river-level in this steep winding lane, turning left for Tadwick at a T-junction after crossing the stream (a tributary of the Avon), then bearing right on the hill at a fork by a stone farmhouse. We have splendid views as we ascend to the top of the hill and turn left for Pennsylvania and Old Sodbury along a major road, but leave it in a few yards for a turning on the right to St Catherine's, passing a reservoir far below in the valley. We continue along this pretty valley to the little manorial group of St Catherine's—the old stone gabled manor-house and church. (Tickets to see the gardens on Thursdays can be obtained from the Pump Room, currently at two shillings.)

Half a mile farther, just beyond the 'Sandy Bank' inn, we turn squarely left for Oakford, climbing uphill again, and in a mile and a half turn right at a T-junction by a park. This brings us shortly to the Roman Foss Way, which we cross left-handed for Colerne and follow the signposts into the pleasant stone-built village with a tall-towered church and a nearby ornamental pillar memorial to Richard Walmesley 'in appreciation of many benevolent acts', dated 1893. Here we turn right past the church for Drewetts Mill, descending a steep hill to the By brook, which we cross beside the old mill and mill house, and climb uphill on the other side to the main road, in which we turn left a difficult turn needing care).

We continue along the main road, passing the R.A.F's Rudloe Manor and Stores, and at the 'Hare and Hounds' inn in Pickwick fork right for Corsham. In the village we turn off at the 'Methuen Arms' to see the fine Elizabethan Corsham Court, with Georgian additions and furniture, and a notable collection of old Masters. It is open to visitors throughout the year, mostly on Wednesdays, Thursdays and Sundays, but from November to March on Sundays only.

We now proceed along the village street, passing some picturesque gabled stone houses, and cross the next main road for Biddestone, continuing to this exceptionally charming village of mellow stone houses with stone roofs round a large village green divided into sections, and a stone-roofed pump near the village pond. We go through the village on the Castle Combe road but just beyond the post office veer left for Gideahall, then shortly left again, this time for Slaughterford. We continue to the last-named village, avoiding a right turn to Ford, as Slaughterford is a pretty riverside settlement worth seeing before we go on to Ford, which is reached by turning right in sight of a telephone box into a narrow close-hedged lane.

We cross the river at Ford, another pretty village, where we turn right at the 'White Hart' inn and right again at the main road, but in about 200 yards turn left for Castle Combe up a steep tree-lined road. Castle Combe has good claims to be one of England's loveliest villages. We enter it alongside the By brook and cross the bridge into the centre with its wonderful old seventeenth-century cottages, stone market cross, church with pinnacled tower, and old manor-house, now a hotel.

Beyond the village we bear left on reaching B4039 towards Badminton, then right in a short quarter of a mile for Grittleton. At the first signposted crossroads we turn left into Grittleton, and at the village crossroads by Grittleton House and the church go forward on the road to Alderton. In about a mile we come to the Foss Way again, and turn right along this ancient straight highway (as usual, all the villages lie off its course) until it suddenly becomes a green track, when we turn right for Norton. We bear left at the next junction and soon reach Norton, which has some fine stone houses, bear left in the village, then right for Malmesbury. Thence we follow the signposts to Malmesbury via Foxley Green, turning right in the main road into Malmesbury. Our way is left for Tetbury at the war memorial, but we must bear right to see the remaining nave of the splendid Norman abbey church, which became the parish church after the dissolution of the monastery. The beautiful recessed Norman arches of the south porch are considered to be among the best Norman work in the country. The famous and magnificent market cross is near the entrance to the abbey. It was built in the fifteenth century and is richly decorated with pinnacles and statues.

Now we proceed to Tetbury, only five miles away, admiring

its Elizabethan town hall on stone pillars in the market place and its old gabled houses as we drive through the town on the Gloucester road. On reaching A433 near the end of the town we turn right for Cirencester but after a mile turn left at the first crossroads for Cherington. We follow the signposts to Cherington and at its little central green turn left towards Avening, keeping left again at the next junction along a pretty valley to the 'Nag's Head' inn, where we turn right. In just over a mile, at Hampton Fields, we bear left then cross a crossroads to a wider road for Minchinhampton.

Minchinhampton, like the other towns we have visited on this tour, was formerly an important wool centre, and it is worth turning right at the crossroads to its centre to see the fine market house on stone pillars, imposing church and the surviving merchants' houses. We avoid the Nailsworth turn as we leave Minchinhampton and soon cross Minchinhampton Common, going through the entrenchments known as 'The Bulwarks'. At a multi-junction we bear left for Rodborough, then follow the Rodborough signposts, looking to Stroud across the Golden Valley of the river Frome. We descend from Rodborough to Stroud, where we can follow the one-way system round the busy town, otherwise turn left on the Gloucester road, B4072, leading to A419 for Stonehouse. We continue to the traffic lights at Cainscross, where we turn left for Dursley on the Bath road, soon leaving this by a right turn, B4066, for Dursley. We climb up to a fine ridge road which goes through a belt of woodland then comes into the open again to give magnificent views to the Vale of Berkeley, the wide Severn, which gleams in the sunlight in fine weather, and the Forest of Dean beyond the river.

After several miles we take the second signposted turning on the left for Nympsfield, also signposted Wotton-under-Edge, and thence follow the signposts towards Wotton, after taking the Tetbury turn at the subsequent junction. Finally we join the main road for a quarter of a mile, then leave it for a turning on the left for Ozleworth, looking down into Tyley Bottom on our right. We bear left at a fork by a tower-like installation for Ozleworth and drive beside Ozleworth Park, descending very steeply, and near the bottom where the road ahead is marked 'Unsuitable for motor vehicles' turn right along the valley—a lovely ride along the shelf.

After two miles we come to a T-junction, where we turn left
for Alderley and Hillesley, going straight on through these
pretty villages to Hawkesbury Upton (left at the fork at the end
of Hillesley). We are now on a wider road climbing on to another
shelf. At the summit is a tall prospect tower, a monument to
General Lord Robert Somerset, who died in 1842, which can be
climbed to see the marvellous views from the top at the cost of
one shilling. Just beyond it we enter Hawkesbury Upton and
continue through the village for Badminton, crossing a main road
beyond it, and following the park wall of Badminton, which we
reach in about a mile. The entrance to Badminton House is in
the village. This fine Palladian mansion, the home of the Dukes
of Beaufort since the seventeenth century, has a fine collection
of paintings and period furniture, and is open to the public from
mid-May to mid-September on Wednesday afternoons, also
Spring Bank Holiday Monday. Badminton is also famous for the
Horse Trials, a three-day event held in April, and the stables and
hunt kennels are open for inspection.

From the 'baronial' village we continue towards Chipping
Sodbury, turning right at the crossroads, and right again at a
clump on to a major road. We continue on this to A46, cross it
for Chipping Sodbury, then take the first turning on the left for
Dodington, following the wall of Dodington Park to the village,
where there is an entrance for pedestrians to Dodington House.
Motorists must drive another mile and a quarter to Dodington
Ash, where we turn left to the entrance and drive through the
lovely park landscaped by 'Capability Brown'. The house is a
lovely Regency mansion with an imposing portico, open to
visitors from May to September on Wednesday, Thursday and
Sunday afternoons, also Bank Holiday Mondays.

From Dodington Ash we turn right along the main road in the
direction of Bath, crossing the M4 motorway, and after a mile turn
right on B4465 for Pucklechurch, and straight on at a subsequent
junction signposted Pucklechurch, but at the next junction turn
left for Dyrham and Doynton, turning left for Dyrham, where
there is yet one more interesting mansion open to visitors,
Dyrham Park, built at the end of the seventeenth century and
scarcely altered since that time. It is open from Easter to
September on Wednesday, Thursday, Friday and Saturday
afternoons, and on Sundays and Bank Holiday Mondays from

12 noon. In October, November, December and March it is open
on Saturday and Sunday afternoons.

We may decide, at this late stage of the tour, to leave this fine
house for another day, in which case we bear right for Doynton,
there going forward for Wick and forking right at the end of the
village by a park wall. Thence we continue to the main road,
turning right in it for Bristol or going straight forward for
Lansdown and Bath.

The second tour, which takes us to the Vale of Berkeley and
Berkeley Castle, and to the cathedral city and county town of
Gloucester, is about the same length as the previous one, i.e.
just over 110 miles. Motorists from Bath can join via A431 to
Bristol, then making for Stapleton on B4058.

From Bristol centre we take the inner circuit past the university
and infirmary, leaving the dual carriageway just beyond a
roundabout for Eastville, Stapleton and Fishponds (this is an
easy way out of the city). We turn right at a major road signposted
Chipping Sodbury, then fork left on B4058 at traffic lights by a
large modern church, our road signposted Stapleton. Continuing
on this pleasant road with the green country in sight, we pass
Stapleton's century-old church, its tower capped by a tall
crocketed spire. A mile beyond on our left we pass Stoke Park
hospital, its buildings looking like a castle on their mound surrounded by woods. Then at Frenchay hospital, which lies on
the right of the road, we take a left fork for Stoke Gifford, soon
leaving all trace of the city behind us. We pass several farms and
farm cottages, going straight on at the first crossroads and avoiding a 'no through road', turning right then left on to a new road
which crosses the M4 and goes under a railway arch (Thornbury
Road). We cross the next major road by a brick field, then
recross the M4.

We continue on this B road towards Thornbury, looking to
the smiling Vale of Berkeley. At the next crossroads we leave the
Thornbury road and go forward on the minor road for Itchington,
reaching it in about a mile, and there at a farm bear right for
Tytherington, a pleasant village group. We bear right at the
church past the 'Swan' inn, right again in half a mile and at a
T-junction by an old toll house turn left; shortly turning right
along Cowship Lane for Wickwar. We go on from there into
Wickwar, once an important centre of the clothing trade, bearing

left on the Kingswood and Wotton road, which passes to the left of the high-set church and goes on towards the Edge (of the Cotswold), which stretches across our horizon. We come to Kingswood in two miles, where it is worth turning right to see the lovely fourteenth-century abbey gatehouse of the old Cistercian monastery founded by William de Berkeley in 1139. The houses beside the gatehouse are built from part of the abbey ruins.

Resuming our road to Wotton-under-Edge, which is literally just that, for it lies immediately under the steep slopes of the western escarpment of the Cotswold, we soon enter this pleasant town with many elegant Georgian houses, including one which has become the police station. The tall-towered church is mainly of the Decorated period, while the fine gabled almshouses date from the seventeenth century. We leave the centre by the Dursley road but after joining a wider road we turn sharp right almost immediately (at the sign Old London Road) uphill through rocks and woods. We are now on Wotton Hill, with an attractive bird's-eye view of Wotton below us in the wide valley and superb views of the Vale of Berkeley and the Severn to the left as we near the summit of the road. The conspicuous monument to our left on Nibley Knoll commemorates William Tyndale, the translator of the Bible, believed to have been born in Nibley in 1484.

This grand road brings us eventually to a major road, in which we bear left for Dursley, our views here stretching as far as the Forest of Dean on the farther side of the Severn, with the village of Uley in the Cam valley below us. At a junction at the top of a steep hill we fork left for Stinchcombe golf course through luxuriant woods and continue along the edge of the hill to a road on the right signposted Dursley. We plunge steeply down this road, rather inappropriately called the Broadway, for which bottom gear is recommended. This takes us into the town of Dursley, where we turn right at the post office, following the one-way system. There is a capacious car park for those who wish to spend a little time in looking round the town, which has a handsome classical market house on pillars with a statue of Queen Anne in front and a spacious fifteenth-century church.

We take B4066 for Stroud after passing the church and follow this road to Uley, which lies under the clearly marked entrenchments of Uleybury hill fort. At a crossroads on the outskirts of

Uley we turn right for Tetbury, climbing on to a plateau from which we look across to Uley grouped round its dominant church. Just after coming out of the woods on to the plateau (less than a quarter of a mile short of a major road) we turn hard left into a narrow lane, passing a farm. Another steep hill, to be taken in low gear, brings us to Owlpen manor-house, a delightful Cotswold stone residence in part dating from the fifteenth century with an adjacent fifteenth-century barn. It is open to the public in June and July on Friday afternoons. Paradoxically the manorial church was rebuilt in the Gothic style in the early part of the nineteenth century.

From the manor-house we drive into Uley, joining the main street near the church and turning right at the little green for Uley Tumulus, reached by a footpath. The key to this Long Barrow with stone chambers is obtained from a cottage (Chetwynd Heights) a quarter of a mile before reaching the barrow, and a modest fee of threepence is the price of access.

We go on to the crossroads after the barrow, where we turn left for Frocester, this road giving us splendid views to the Severn and beyond, with Berkeley Castle a prominent landmark in the Vale. Frocester has venerable associations. The old monastic tithe barn, one of the largest in England, is well preserved and Frocester Court is an ancient manor-house, visited by Queen Elizabeth in 1574. At the centre of the village we turn right by the 'George' inn for Leonard Stanley, where the priory church of St Leonard, an early twelfth-century structure with original Norman work, is reached by a short detour to the right opposite the post office. There are a few fragments of the Austin priory incorporated in the nearby farm buildings. We can go on past the church to rejoin our road at the 'Lamb' inn. Otherwise we go straight on for King's Stanley, with the curving wooded edge of the Wold to our right.

At King's Stanley we turn left for Stroud, soon passing the towered church standing among the neat clipped yews in the churchyard, then crossing the river Frome and the Stroudwater Canal before coming to the major road T-junction where we turn right for Stroud. On reaching the traffic lights at Cainscross we turn left for Cashes Green and Randwick, and at the end of the houses of Cashes Green go straight on past the school at the junction, and at the next junction turn left for Randwick, where just beyond its church a steep hill leads to the National Trust property of Standish Woods. On joining a wider road we continue to a T-junction by Stockend Wood (also in the care of the National Trust), where we turn right on the Gloucester road.

At the village of Edge we join a major road to Gloucester, only six miles distant, into which we drive. Gloucester is a handsome city of ancient foundation. Even before the Romans there was a settlement of the Iberians here, which the Romans later fortified and named it Colonia Glevum. Its most impressive link with the past is the magnificent cathedral founded as the church of the Benedictine monastery dating from 681. It retains its Norman core and the additions of later ages are skilfully blended into the present harmonious composition richly decorated inside and crowned by the beautiful central tower. The cloisters are exceptionally fine, with exquisite fan vaulting. Among the many venerable monuments the elaborate tomb of the murdered Edward II is the most striking, the stone effigy of the King lying under a lofty canopy of delicate arches and pinnacles. His body was brought here from Berkeley Castle in 1327 after it had been refused burial at Bristol and Malmesbury. In addition there are other ancient churches in the town, the timbered fifteenth century 'New Inn', with its picturesque galleried courtyard, and a number of interesting old houses. All in all, Gloucester demands an hour or two's exploration.

We leave the town by the Bristol road, A38, as far as the outskirts of Quedgeley, then turn right in the road signposted Elmore (a quarter of a mile beyond the point where the Ring road joins our road on the left), shortly crossing the Gloucester and Berkeley Canal by a swingbridge. In another quarter of a mile we reach the bank of the broad Severn, which our road closely follows for half a mile. When we leave it we soon come to a T-junction where we turn right for Elmore and Longney, passing some ancient black and white timber-framed houses, then turn left for Elmore church and Longney. We soon pass the lovely wrought-iron entrance of Elmore Court, the seat of the Guise family since the time of Henry III. It is a beautiful house, mainly Elizabethan, though additions were made in the seventeenth and eighteenth centuries, and there is medieval work in the cellars. The house is open to the public on Sunday afternoons from 1 May to 31 August and on Bank Holidays.

Thence we go on to Longney, driving beside orchards to this long-established fruit-growing centre by the banks of Severn. We go through the straggling village as far as its church, just beyond which we turn right for Saul, passing the quaintly-named 'Plate of Elvers' inn. The way to Saul runs through more orchards and beside the bank of the wide river for some distance, and we finally cross the Stroudwater Canal into Saul, there going on for Frampton. We cross the Gloucester and Berkeley Canal, the way signposted Stonehouse at the crossing, before we arrive at Frampton, where the village and medieval church beside the wide green make a picturesque composition. Beyond the village we soon come to A38, where we turn right on this straight road, formerly part of the Roman road from Gloucester to Bristol. We follow it through Cambridge and past the turn to the Wild Fowl Trust, half a mile beyond which we turn right for Gossington, going forward at the first junction for Halmore. At the T-junction at Halmore we turn left, then immediately right for Berkeley, turning left at the major road after a mile, which takes us into this historic town.

The entrance to the castle is beyond the 'Berkeley Arms'. It is one of the most interesting of the historic castles to which the public are admitted. It was built in the middle of the twelfth century and is claimed to be the oldest inhabited castle in England, still in the possession of the Berkeley family. Not only are we shown the historic keep, its breach a silent witness to its part in the Civil War, and the room and dungeon below where King Edward II was imprisoned and finally murdered, the great hall and other state rooms, but we are able to see the medieval kitchen and buttery, which give a fascinating picture of daily life in the fourteenth century. The castle is open every afternoon except Monday from 1 April to 30 September, but all day on Bank Holiday Mondays, also on Sunday afternoons in October.

From the castle we continue on the Bristol road, forking right in less than half a mile for Hill, reaching it in less than three miles. There we turn right for Oldbury, following the signposts to this village and turning left at its post office for Kington. We are still among apple orchards as we drive to Kington, thence going on to Thornbury. Its handsome church is to the left of the town and near it is Thornbury Castle, begun by the ill-fated Duke of Buckingham who was beheaded by order of Henry VIII.

Although it is not open to the public we can get a glimpse of this striking mansion.

We retrace our way from the church and castle and enter the town, a pleasant market centre, quaint features being the large swan and lion facing each other across the main street, signs of the 'Swan' hotel and 'White Lion' inn respectively. We go right through the town and continue on a tree-lined and wooded road to a crossroads at Alveston, turning right on B4461 for Aust, and right again in a quarter of a mile for Elberton, following the signposts to the latter village. We now go on to Aust, going under the M4 and then following the signposts to Aust Ferry and continuing on B4055 along a grand riverside boulevard (ample parking) with fine views across the river to Chepstow and the coast of Wales, and the Severn bridge to our right. B4055 brings us to the 'Cross Hands' inn, where we turn right at the T-junction for Severn Beach and follow the signposts to this small resort on the estuary. At the station we turn left over the level crossing, then right on the other side for Avonmouth.

After passing an enormous number of oil storage tanks and installations we go forward thankfully for Henbury among green fields and hedgerows again, passing through Hallen, and at Henbury T-junction turn right. The entrance to Blaise Castle, which offers the attractions of a camp, folk museum and gorge, is on our left and we drive alongside the park and past the car park, then through woods. We cross the first crossroad for Stoke Bishop and can go forward into Bristol at this point, but it is pleasant to turn right at the next crossing by traffic lights as for Avonmouth, then left at the next traffic lights on A4, which runs alongside the Avon—a green way through the Avon Gorge into Bristol centre, and thence to Bath if our start was from there.

CHAPTER FOUR

THE SOMERSET PLAIN AND
VALE OF TAUNTON DEANE

THE TOURS IN THIS CHAPTER take us south, as far as the Vale of
Taunton Deane with Taunton as its centre, and to the Wiltshire
and Dorset borders, starting from the market town of Yeovil,
and we explore in detail the Somerset plain, visiting its
most historic town, Glastonbury, described as the cradle of
British Christianity. The first tour is routed from Bath and, of
course, Bristol motorists can join by driving to Bath. From
Bath the total distance covered is approximately 95 miles, so
that if the start is from Bristol the distance will be about 120
miles.

We leave Bath by Bathwick Hill and at the top of the hill turn
left for Claverton, passing the late Georgian Claverton Manor,
the home of the American Museum in Britain. The completely
furnished rooms contain exhibits of every phase of American
domestic life from the seventeenth to the mid-nineteenth century,
and can be visited from Easter to mid-October daily in the
afternoon except Mondays, though it is open on Bank Holiday
Mondays. We turn right at the main road at Claverton but leave
it in less than two miles at the approach to Limpley Stoke, where
we turn left on B3108 for Bradford-on-Avon, crossing the Avon
and the Kennet and Avon Canal.

This B road takes us into Bradford-on-Avon in just over two
miles, and we drive into the centre of this picturesque riverside
town, for long famous for the manufacture of broadcloth. Its
unique heritage is the old Saxon church of St Lawrence, for
centuries desecrated and used for other purposes, such as a
schoolhouse, and hemmed in by later buildings. In the middle
of the nineteenth century it was re-discovered and carefully
restored and today is a near-perfect example of a Saxon church,
with nave, chancel and north porch (the south porch has

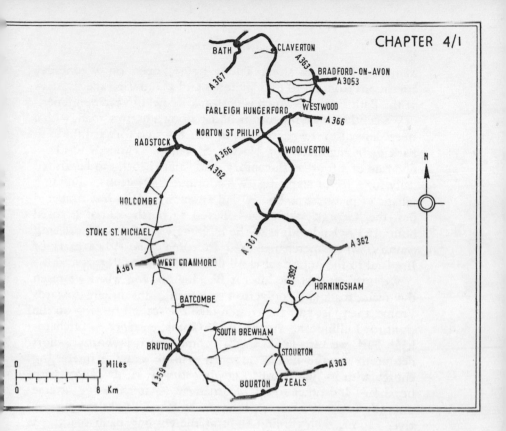

disappeared). The parish church also dates from early times and has Norman work as well as features of all periods of Gothic architecture.

That is not the end of Bradford's interest for, in addition to its many fine stone houses, some dating back to the fifteenth century, and groups of almshouses, the town bridge over the Avon retains its medieval bridge chapel, at which travellers paused to give thanks for a safe crossing. Only three other such chapels exist to the present day, at St Ives in Huntingdonshire, and at Wakefield and Rotherham in Yorkshire.

We cross the bridge for Frome and bear right on B3109 again for Frome, soon passing the great tithe barn, yet one more of Bradford's links with the past, which has been in constant use as a barn since the fourteenth century. Next we cross the Kennet and Avon Canal and in less than half a mile fork right for West-wood, going forward in a wider road into the village but at the 'New Inn' bear left towards the church and nearby Westwood

Manor. This is a stone Tudor house, open on Wednesday afternoons from April to September and also during the ten days of the Bath Festival, which is customarily held in early summer.

We continue past the manor-house along a narrow road, with a steep descent to the main road, in which we go forward through Farleigh Hungerford for Norton St Philip. Farleigh Castle, a fine ruin of a fourteenth-century castle and chapel, can be visited daily for a fee of sixpence. We continue to Norton St Philip, a village of picturesque houses and an exceptionally fine timbered inn, the 'George', which is believed to be the oldest licensed house in England. Most of the building dates from the fifteenth century, when merchants used to come from other parts of England to the important cloth fair held in the village.

We turn left past the inn for Beckington, and when we reach the main road at Woolverton we turn right briefly towards Frome, then just past the church take the second turning on the right for Lullington. At the mock Gothic entrance to Orchard-leigh Park we turn left towards Frome, but it is worth a short detour to see the model 'baronial' village and the interesting church with its fine Norman north doorway, richly carved with beakheads and other forms of ornament. After that we resume our way towards Frome, passing a large mill and crossing the river Frome, then turning right at the ensuing main road. At the approach to the town, which we visit on another tour (page 10), we turn left for Warminster and follow the signposts towards it, passing one of Frome's cloth factories.

The wooded hills of Longleat Park and its surrounding country are now imminent, and when we reach the entrance we must not miss seeing the splendid late Elizabethan house with its fine state rooms, paintings and period furniture. The house and park are open every day of the year except Christmas Day, and among its attractions is a lion safari, where visitors may drive among the lions roaming freely in part of the park and study them at close quarters. The park is beautifully landscaped, the stream running though it, the Longa Leta, dammed and widened to form a series of lakes.

If we are not seeing the house on this occasion, we take the road for Horningsham at the park gates, driving through pine trees and rhododendrons, at the entrance to Heaven's Gate going straight on to Horningsham. In the village we continue past the church, skirting the park and soon bearing right for Frome. At the 'Bath Arms' we continue for Frome, and if we are coming from the house we shortly join this road at a little triangular green. At the foot of a wooded hill we again turn right towards Frome, then we take the first turning on the left, signposted Witham Friary. When we reach a railway we turn left for Gare Hill, driving towards the line of wooded hills again. Rhododendrons and pine trees line the road, and later silver birches and other trees, and we pass the little church near the summit of Gare Hill, looking all the more attractive because of its position.

At a junction a mile and a quarter beyond the church we go forward for Bruton and continue towards it at the next crossing road. The long views on our right over the vale of Somerset are very beautiful and as we drop there are views also to the left and ahead, with low wooded hills flattening out towards the Vale of Blackmore. Alfred's Tower, on Kingsettle Hill above Stourhead, is a prominent landmark now visible. We continue to the foot of the hill through a hamlet, then turn left as for Bruton past an inn as the road starts to climb, shortly turning left for Charlton Musgrove. This takes us through the pretty riverside village of South Brewham, and we follow this wider road for a full mile from South Brewham until we reach a turning on the left signposted King Alfred's Tower. We climb steeply towards the tower, a lovely ride, and pass right beside the tower (where there is a spacious picnic place).

We emerge from the woods to open fields and bear right at a junction, and right again in a subsequent wider road. Now we follow the signposts to Stourhead, descending to the lake and Stourton village. It is a most beautiful vista, a strange feature of which is the old High Cross of Bristol, originally erected at Bristol's central crossroads in 1373, which is impressively floodlit after dark. The romantic pleasure grounds laid out around the lake and diversified with classical temples are open daily all the year, while the early Georgian Palladian house, with some fine paintings and Chippendale furniture designed for the house, is open all the year on Wednesday, Saturday, Sunday and Bank Holiday afternoons, also on Thursday afternoon from March to October.

We continue beside the lake to Zeals, and at Zeals church, a spired modern edifice, we reach A303 and turn right in it through

Bourton. Just over a mile beyond Bourton's towered church,
also modern, we fork right on B3081 for Bruton, and are now in
the midst of low hills. We continue to Bruton but at a fork it is
worth making a detour through the pretty little village of
Stoney Stoke along a lane which rejoins B3081. At the approach
to Bruton we fork left into a minor road to see the abbey dovecot,
skirting the old wall of the abbey. The stone dovecot stands on a
high mound, from which there is a grand view over the town.

Bruton, into which we turn near the foot of the hill, is one of
the most interesting towns in the county, and deserves thorough
exploration. Its fine church was formerly the minster of the
abbey and is a magnificent Perpendicular structure with a tall
tower richly decorated in the typical Somerset style. We pass the
King Edward VI Grammar School on the way to the church,
and near the school is an old packhorse bridge over the river
Brue known as Bruton Bow. At the church we turn left over the
river, then left again beside a beautiful Georgian house to go
down the High Street to see Sexey's Almshouses, founded in
1638. The houses and chapel are built round a courtyard and are
exceptionally attractive. The old Abbey Court House (now a
private house), is on the same side of the High Street just short of
the almshouses.

We return down the High Street, and proceed on the Shepton
Mallet road, passing many other Georgian and earlier houses in
the town, but after about a quarter of a mile fork right for
Batcombe. This road takes us straight to Batcombe in just over
two miles, and at its impressive church with a splendid Somerset
tower we turn left through the pretty village for Cranmore. We
follow the signposts to Cranmore, with fine views to our left
across the Alham valley to a range of low hills on the other side,
the landscape dotted with young and mature trees. Just before
we cross the railway into West Cranmore we pass the fine
Southill House on our right. We pass West Cranmore church,
another with a good Somerset tower, and cross A361 for Waterlip
and Stoke St Michael. We follow the signposts to the latter
village (later the way is signposted Bath) and pass the vast
Moons Hill quarries before entering Stoke St Michael, turning
left there at the 'Knatchbull Arms' short of the church, described
by one critic as an example of 'architectural depravity'.

In less than half a mile after this we turn right for Holcombe

Bristol's market cross
(1373), now at
Stourton.
(Chapter 4.)

The lake and pleasure
gardens, Stourhead.
(Chapter 4.)

The medieval 'George' inn, Norton St Philip.   (Chapter 4.)

Sexey's Almshouses, founded 1638, in Bruton High Street.   (Chapter 4.)

(the road past the church also joins this road) and in Holcombe go straight through the village for Radstock, to which we now continue. From here we can continue to Bath on A367 (8 miles) but a pleasant alternative is to turn left off the main road after just over half a mile for Clandown, going through the village and crossing a major road beyond it. We cross a second cross-road after another mile, then descend a steep hill to a village by the Cam brook, on the other side of which we turn right for Tunley. We bear right again for Tunley at the next signposted junction, then the road takes us straight into Bath, joining the main road a mile and a half beyond Tunley.

Our next tour is routed from Yeovil, an important industrial town and agricultural centre. It is a largely modern town, showing little sign of its long history apart from the parish church of St John the Baptist at its centre, a noble and beautiful church with lofty Perpendicular windows which was built in the latter part of the fourteenth century on the site of an earlier church. Yeovil is situated in the midst of lovely country and is a good centre with ample accommodation for tourists. The tour, which takes us across the Somerset plain to Glastonbury and other historic places, is little more than 100 miles in length.

We leave the town centre by A30 and after crossing the railway and passing a factory complex on the outskirts we soon reach the river Yeo and after crossing it climb up a wooded hill. Halfway up this hill we turn right for Bradford Abbas, driving through a rock gorge, but we avoid the next turn to Bradford Abbas and go forward for Sherborne, less than three miles distant on this road. Sherborne is the first of several historic towns visited on this tour. It has a famous abbey and school, originally founded, it is said, in the eighth century and claiming King Alfred as a pupil. The school incorporates some of the old abbey buildings. The abbey church is a magnificent one, a Norman building fundamentally, but rebuilt and enlarged in the Perpendicular style in the fifteenth century. The old almshouses, refounded in 1437, and the abbey conduit in Cheap Street, a beautiful fourteenth-century structure, are both worth finding. The old castle, now only a ruined fragment, is on the hill outside the town to the south-east.

We leave the town centre by A30, following this as far as Milborne Port, where after passing the church, noting its massive

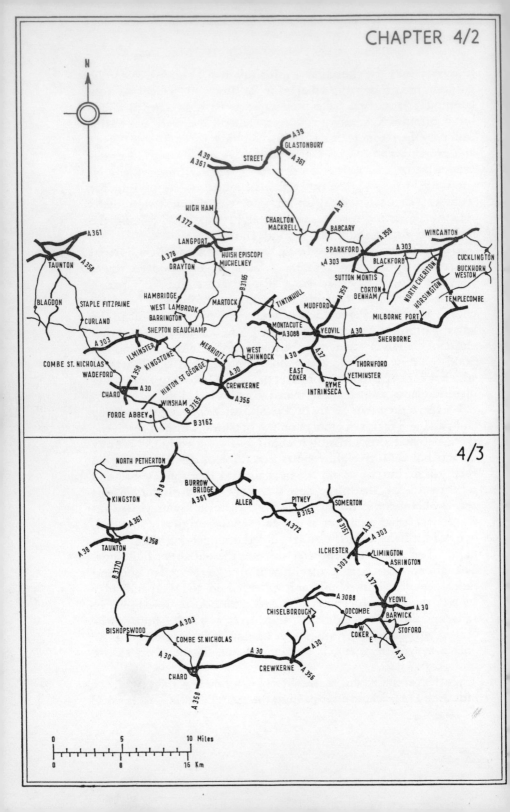

square tower, we turn left by the market house for Charlton
Horethorne. After a short quarter of a mile, however, we turn
right at a crossroads in the built-up area, immediately leaving the
town and soon climbing up a low wooded hill and over the
ridge, with good views to the left. When we are joined by
another road on the left we veer right away from the ridge and
descend into the valley. At the next junction we fork left, away
from Henstridge, for Templecombe, and on reaching the main
road in Templecombe turn left on the Wincanton road for about
200 yards, then right for Buckhorn Weston, to which we continue. In the village we turn left for Cucklington, keeping left on
the outskirts of the village, and straight on at the next junction
(avoiding the Gillingham turn), then at a T-junction left on to the
Cucklington ridge as far as Cucklington church, which has an
unusual south tower, rebuilt after being damaged in the great
storm of 1703. Here we go forward for Wincanton, looking
across the wide valley from the cliff, and thence follow the
Wincanton signposts.

Wincanton is a largely modern town, with little interest for
the antiquarian, so there is no need to enter the centre (except
for shopping) and we turn left on the outskirts where Buckhorn
Weston is signposted and continue towards the latter at the next
junction. This takes us over the northern marches of the fertile
Vale of Blackmore and after a mile we turn right for Horsington,
crossing the river Cale. A fine Georgian house in the distance
heralds the approach to Horsington, a charming village with
another handsome Georgian house beside the church, Horsington
House (now one of Dr Barnardo's homes). Opposite the entrance
to the house is the shaft of a medieval cross with the remains of a
carved figure.

We turn right in the main road by the mill at the end of the
village, shortly passing the decorative 'White Horse' inn, and
continue to North Cheriton, where we turn left through the
stone-built village up to the church and right beside the old
stocks outside the churchyard, climbing steeply to another ridge.
On reaching B3145 we cross it left-handed for Maperton and
continue to this small village group, its church half hidden by the
old manor-house, just beyond which we turn left, then shortly
right, for Blackford. At Blackford church we go forward over
the crossroads for Compton Pauncefoot (or Pauncefote). We go

through an orchard and bear left at the next junction, signposted Sherborne, driving alongside the estate of Compton Castle, of which we have a good view, also of its lake, from our road in just over a quarter of a mile.

We continue along the ridge, with extensive views on our left to Bulbarrow Hill and the north Dorset downs, and later on our right over the Yeo valley. As we descend we bear right at a fork for Corton Denham and right again in a few yards, and are soon in this village under the steep Corton Hill which ends at the Beacon (646 ft). We drive along the valley under the slopes of the Beacon and climb over a low pass. Ahead of us is the great earthwork of Cadbury Castle, believed to be the site of King Arthur's Camelot and on which excavation is being carried out in the hope of finding tangible evidence. We turn right towards the earthwork, where South Cadbury is signposted, then left at a T-junction for Sutton Montis, turning left at the village T-junction for Sparkford. We drive through the attractive little village of Weston Bampfylde, unmistakable because of its unusual octagonal church tower. From there it is only half a mile to Sparkford church, a late Georgian Gothic one rebuilt on to a medieval tower. We go on through the village to the main road, there left for 100 yards, then over a railway bridge and immediately right for South Barrow beside the park boundary of Sparkford Hall, of which there is a good view through gaps in the trees. Short of South Barrow we fork left for Babcary along a narrow hedged lane over level country with numerous trees, especially elms.

At a T-junction in Babcary we turn left for Charlton Mackrell, then right at the old 'Red Lion' inn, soon reaching the Foss Way, where we turn left towards Ilchester. Neglecting two Charlton Mackrell turns we continue on this Roman road as far as the A372 crossing road where we turn right for Langport and in a short quarter of a mile we take the turning for Charlton Mackrell this time, which is also signposted Lytes Cary. The entrance to this fine fifteenth-century manor-house, with a chapel dating from the first half of the fourteenth century, is on our right in about half a mile. It is open to visitors on Wednesday and Saturday afternoons from March to October.

From there we go on to Charlton Mackrell, at the junction there going forward for Street, crossing a main road for Glastonbury in just over a mile. At the next junction, however, we go

straight on towards Street again through a large tract of woodland, with some new forestry, and as we drive over the high
ridge we reach a magnificent viewpoint (with a parking place),
where we look out on the left across King's Sedge Moor to the
easily recognizable landmarks of Ham Hill and Dundon Hill,
with Dundon village below, and the low range of the Polden
Hills to our right. The column on Windmill Hill is a monument
to Sir Samuel Hood, the famous admiral who served under
Nelson. He was described by Nelson as 'the best officer that
England has to boast of'. There is another parking place near
this monument, from which we can look across Glastonbury
Plain to the Tor and beyond to the long line of the Mendip Hills.

Just beyond the monument we turn right for Butleigh Wootton
and at a subsequent junction left for Glastonbury, thence following the signposts to this historic town. Identified with the Island
of Avalon, King Arthur's burial place, its links with Christianity
go back even farther, for the legend is that Joseph of Arimathea
came here with eleven disciples, bringing with him the Holy
Grail from the Last Supper, and that they built a little church of
wattle and daub. This tiny hallowed site was the nucleus round
which many later churches were built, including that of St Peter
and St Paul in the early eighth century under King Ina, who
was a great benefactor of the church and monastery. Dunstan was
Abbot of Glastonbury at the end of the tenth century and was
responsible for building a larger stone church. Then with the
coming of the Normans began the building of the beautiful
church and monastic quarters. Although there was a disastrous
fire in 1184, the abbey was rebuilt, and it is from this rebuilding
and the later additions that the present ruins date, of which the
most interesting are the chapel of St Joseph and the Abbot's
kitchen. In the grounds there are several specimens of the Holy
Thorn, claimed to be descendants of the thorn staff of Joseph,
which miraculously sprouted when he stuck it in the ground
and blossomed every Christmas Day.

The entrance to the abbey (a small fee is charged for admission)
is opposite the 'George' hotel, an early pilgrims' inn built in the
late fifteenth century by the then Abbot. There are other interesting churches in the town and in the High Street the Tribunal,
the fifteenth-century court house of the Abbey, admits visitors
daily at a fee of sixpence. The Abbey Barn is in Chilkwell Street,

a vast gabled building with figures of the four Evangelists at the four corners.

We shall leave this shrine of early Christianity with regret, taking the Bridgwater Road, A39, also signposted Street. We drive through the long straggling town of Street, bearing left for Somerton on B3151. We follow this road as far as the Polden Hills (now in the care of the National Trust), where we turn right at a crossroads on the summit by a prominent clump of pine trees, our road signposted Ashcott. This is a fine ridge way with extensive views on both sides. We continue along the ridge towards Ashcott until we reach a main road, A361, in which we turn left towards Taunton, and after a mile turn left in Pedwell village for High Ham over King's Sedge Moor, the scene of Monmouth's rebellion against King James II. Numerous ditches drain the level land, which is broken up by the numerous willow trees which line the roads and dykes.

As we approach the Ham Hills we turn right a quarter of a mile short of them in a narrow willow-lined road, currently unsignposted, driving parallel with the hills at first, then veering towards the nose, at a fork taking an unpromising track which climbs round the nose to give a fine view across west Somerset to the Quantocks. Near the top of Turn Hill we veer left uphill to the actual summit, where a gate on the left leads to a National Trust viewpoint. Immediately beyond this we take a left fork to High Ham and soon reach the village. The church of St Andrew is a handsome late Perpendicular building with a beautifully carved roof, rood screen and pews, and has some intriguing gargoyles, particularly those of Darby and Joan above the porch. From the village green we take the Langport road, thence following the signposts to Langport (neglecting a turn signposted Muchelney).

In Langport we turn left by a handsome Georgian house, now a post office, up a steep hill past the church with a tall pinnacled tower, just beyond it passing under an archway over the road above which is a medieval structure known as the Hanging Chapel. This building was used as a grammar school from 1675 onwards. The village of Huish Episcopi adjoins Langport and in half a mile we reach its famous church, which has one of the most beautiful towers in Somerset, richly ornamented with elaborate pierced work and crowned by graceful pinnacles. The south door is a fine

Norman one, curiously coloured red as a result of an ancient fire.

At the church we bear right for Muchelney, another old village full of architectural interest. An abbey was founded here in Saxon times and the plan of the abbey church and some of the medieval monastic buildings in a good state of preservation may be seen daily throughout the year (admission fee sixpence). The parish church is also a medieval building with the typical Somerset tower, and near the church is the ancient Vicarage House and village cross. We turn right at the church on the Drayton road and continue on this into Drayton, noting the fine old churchyard cross with a sculptured figure of St Michael slaying the dragon beside a yew tree as we pass the church. Just beyond the church we turn left, then in just over a quarter of a mile right for Hambridge. On reaching B3168 we turn left towards Ilminster, crossing the river Isle just before going through Hambridge, then at the 'Westport' inn bearing left for Barrington. This is an attractive long village with many thatched cottages, at the end of which a 'no through road' leads to the lovely Tudor Barrington Court, a National Trust property open to visitors on Wednesdays all through the year.

We resume our road through Barrington, passing the hall on our left and the Tudor manor-house on our right. Then the road goes through an ivy-clad rock cutting bordered with ferns, and in the midst of this cutting we turn left for Shepton Beauchamp and at a subsequent junction go straight on through the village towards Langport, going through West Lambrook, beyond which we leave the Langport road for East Lambrook, turning right when we reach that village. East Lambrook Manor (right) with its cottage garden is open to visitors on Thursday afternoons from May to July and in September.

We continue on this road to a T-junction, where we turn left towards Yeovil, at the next junction proceeding towards Somerton, and then into Martock. This is another small market town with some fine ancient buildings. It has a handsome Renaissance market hall, a market cross with a sundial and weather vane dated 1741, and nearby is the seventeenth-century manor-house. The church is a magnificent one, mostly in the Perpendicular style, the tower less elaborate than many we have seen on this tour, but an attractive feature is the fine pierced parapet. Inside, the beautiful carved oak roof decorated with angels is worth

seeing. Near the church is the fourteenth-century rectory and
the old grammar school.

We leave the town by driving to the right of the market
house and past the 'White Hart' inn, then bearing left for Yeovil.
Thereafter we make for Tintinhull, turning left on the next main
road, the Foss Way. We neglect the first turning to Tintinhull
but turn right to it at the next crossroads. Tintinhull House is
signposted in the village along a 'no through road'. It is a
seventeenth-century manor-house with a lovely garden open to
the public on Wednesday and Saturday afternoons from April to
October, also on Bank Holiday Mondays, and the gardens are
open in addition on Thursday afternoons. We return to the
village street and resume our way, bearing right past the green,
noting the stocks under the ancient elm, also passing the church
and the fine old rectory.

We turn right at the next junction to take us back to the Foss
Way, and turn left along it as far as a crossroads where Stoke is
signposted to the left. We turn into Stoke, soon passing on our
right Parsonage (or Priory) Farm, where there is an old chantry
house with a bell cote where the priests resided, also a circular
dovecot, reached through a Tudor arch (the chantry has long
since disappeared). We turn left at the main street and then in a
few yards right signposted Ham (Hamdon) Hill. At the summit
there is an immense British camp, which the Romans later
occupied, and there are numerous later quarries (the stone is
excellent for building). It is worth parking for a few minutes to
enjoy the immense views and identify the various features of the
panorama spread before us.

We keep straight on, neglecting a left fork which leads to
Montacute, and going through a rock cutting, then over the next
crossroads for Yeovil, joining A30 into the town.

Our third tour is routed from Taunton, an important residential
and touring centre, and covers a total distance of just under 90
miles. Favourably situated on the river Tone in the midst of the
fertile Vale of Taunton Deane, it has not only developed as the
leading commercial and market town of Somerset but has also
become increasingly popular as a touring base, with good
accommodation to suit all pockets. It has famous public schools,
a magnificent parish church and a restored castle on the site of
the one originally established by King Ina early in the eighth

century. The great hall of the castle is now used as a museum, while the outer gateway known as the Castle Bow is incorporated in the 'Castle' hotel. The extensive library, which contains many books of reference relating to Somerset, is also housed in the castle buildings.

In the market place, where the ill-fated Duke of Monmouth was proclaimed king in 1685, there are several ancient buildings, among which is the gabled Tudor house, its elaborate timber work typical of the sixteenth century. By a strange coincidence, the town was taken by an earlier pretender to the throne, Perkin Warbeck, during his rebellion of 1497. He was soon routed by the forces of King Henry VII and met the same fate as that of the luckless Duke nearly two centuries later.

We leave the town centre by A38, the Bristol road, then turn right on B3170 for Honiton, continuing to a junction where Staple Fitzpaine is signposted and take this left turn and follow the signposts to Staple Fitzpaine. By the beautiful tower of its church we turn left for Ashill and at the next crossroads right for Curland. Here we turn left at the green triangle by the village post office, then right for Ilminster. We go straight on to Ilminster on this road, turning left on joining the main road into it. We follow the Ilchester road through upper Ilminster and at the end of the town fork right for Kingstone. (The only notable buildings in Ilminster, formerly an important market town, are the splendid church and nearby grammar school bearing the date 1586.)

In the small settlement of Kingstone we turn left for Crewkerne, passing the pleasant little church on our left then going forward for Allowenshay along a lane between high banks. We soon reach this little village group and turn right just past a telephone box, our road still a narrow one between high banks. We turn left at the next T-junction, then go forward at the two following junctions to Hinton St George. We go forward once more in the next hamlet, half encircling a wooded hill and climbing up to a shelf road commanding long views. The village of Hinton St George is a charming one, with an old Tudor manor-house opposite the fine church. We drive straight through the village and on reaching A356 turn right then left in 100 yards for Martock, immediately going through the village of Merriott, passing the church and some interesting old houses. At the

T-junction towards the end of the village we turn left, the way again signposted Martock, but at the subsequent T-junction turn right in distinctive broken hill country. In less than a quarter of a mile we bear left in a minor road for the Chinnocks, bearing left again at the first fork into West Chinnock and left by the church into the wider village road past a charming row of cottages. At the end of the village we fork left, signposted Martock, but at a subsequent junction right for Chiselborough, where in sight of the handsome spire of the church we turn right for Norton-sub-Hamdon. As we drive towards Hamdon Hill we have one of the best views of the entrenchments on its summit.

At a junction signposted Hamdon Hill we go forward and soon reach a shelf on its west side overlooking the plain to the Quantocks, the Mendips and beyond them to Exmoor. On reaching a main road we turn right by a Tudor house and continue to Montacute, passing an entrance to the noble Elizabethan Montacute House. The visitors' entrance is farther on past the church, and the house is open daily except Tuesday from 1 March until 31 October (Wednesday, Saturday and Sunday afternoons in February, November and December 1–23). Among the mellow old houses in the square is that of Robert Sherborne, the last prior of the former Cluniac priory, of which a beautiful fifteenth-century gatehouse survives beside the church.

From Montacute we take the Yeovil road and after crossing the railway, and neglecting the first turning to Lufton, we take the second turning on the left beside a housing estate attached to a military base. At the first crossroads we turn right for Yeovil, subsequently crossing several minor and major roads (motorists from Yeovil can join the tour by turning right from any of these crossing roads out of the town). Our road is variously signposted Marston Magna, Wincanton and Mudford, the last named being the only one on our route. Beyond Mudford, a mainly modern town, we cross the river Yeo, then take the first turning on the right for Sherborne and follow the signposts to it. In Sherborne (see page 41) we take the Dorchester road, Cheap Street, and after going over a level crossing turn right by Sherborne Park, then at the end of the cliff go forward for Thornford and Yetminster.

We drive through the old village of Thornford, distinguished by a stone clock tower in its centre, and proceed on this high road, which commands long views in all directions, to Yetminster. At the crossroads in Yetminster we turn right for Ryme Intrinseca and in this little village, of which the most distinctive feature is its name, we turn right on the road signposted Yeovil. In under a mile we cross a major road for East Coker and continue to this lovely village, with its exceptional group of hall, church and almshouses. The hall, Coker Court, dates from the fifteenth century, while the row of almshouses on the road to the hall and church are of seventeenth-century foundation.

Beyond the village we turn left for West Coker and at a crossroads in a sandstone gorge turn left again, signposted Hardington. We continue to this hillside village and at the church turn left, then shortly right for Crewkerne, turning left at the main road into Crewkerne. The buildings in this small town are mainly modern, the stone market house bearing the date 1900, but it has a handsome church and nearby is the old grammar school, founded in 1499.

We leave Crewkerne by A30 and just beyond the end of the town and the last houses, halfway up a hill, we turn left into an obscure unsignposted lane, soon crossing a major road for Hewish. We keep right at the next junction by a group of cottages, and turn sharp right about 100 yards farther. Here, unbelievably, we are almost 800 ft up, with splendid views in every direction. At the next crossroads we turn left for Winsham and we soon descend gradually into this winding village of many pretty houses and cottages. We go straight over the crossroads beside its old market cross for Forde Abbey and continue to this unique monastic survival, which is open to visitors on Wednesdays from May to September, and on a number of Sundays during those months. The Cistercian abbey was founded in the twelfth century, the great hall and tower built in 1500 by the last abbot, and after the dissolution most of the fine exterior was maintained. Among its treasures are the famous Raphael tapestries, woven at Mortlake.

We continue on the same road, from which there is a distant view of the abbey if we are unable to visit it on this occasion, and at the next junction we turn right into the Chard road. After crossing a level crossing we turn left briefly towards Axminster then right again for Chard, and right at a church on reaching a main road. We enter Chard on the Taunton road and turn left at the fine Tudor building up the High Street of the old town, then just past the town hall turn right, signposted Combe St Nicholas. In the High Street there are several ancient buildings, notably the 'Choughs' inn and 'Tudor Court', (1580).

We follow the high-set road through Wadeford to Combe St Nicholas, where we bear right for Taunton and forward at the next two crossroads again for Taunton, the second, A303, left-handed. Here we are nearly 1,000 ft up and from this road look across to the Brendon Hills and the outliers of Exmoor. At a junction 6½ miles from Taunton we bear left for Wellington over Staple Hill. Our views are now mainly to the south and on a clear day the sea is visible down the Axe valley. We cross the next main road, still in the direction of Wellington, and now the Quantocks and Mendips come into view on our right. At the next main road crossing, however, we turn right for Blagdon and Taunton, with a remarkable view of Taunton down in the vale. This last part of the ride is a wonderful scenic return to our base.

The last tour is routed from Yeovil, but can be equally well followed from Taunton, through which the tour passes. It takes us across the county as far as the Quantock Hills and covers a distance of about 100 miles. We leave the centre of Yeovil by A30 towards London but turn right to the station opposite the 'Elephant and Castle' (Newton Road), crossing the railway beside the station and climbing up a hill through ivy-clad sandstone cliffs, looking down on the river Yeo on our left. At the top of the hill we go forward for Yeovil Junction and soon come into the little village of Stoford, its cottages stone and thatched. We bear right at the green for Barwick, keeping left at a subsequent junction and later coming to A37, in which we turn right, then left in 100 yards, our way signposted Sutton Bingham.

In just under a mile we turn right for the Cokers, first driving through the winding street of thatched cottages beside a little stream in East Coker (page 51), then turning left for West Coker. Beyond the turning, on the other side of a bridge and on the right of the road, is an ancient house, formerly the manor-house, with a Gothic porch and windows. This was the birthplace in 1652 of the famous navigator, William Dampier. We soon reach the centre of West Coker, where there is another ancient manor-house, with medieval chimneys, dating from the fourteenth century, on our right. When we reach the main road we turn right and at the end of the village turn left immediately into an unsignposted lane, and left again at a T-junction on the ridge. We follow this ridge road, with extensive views on either side, to the village of Odcombe, marked by its high-set church, and there go straight on, steering towards Hamdon Hill and climbing to the top, avoiding right turns to Montacute. We drive through the entrenchments and quarry workings and at the small car park on the summit turn sharply left, with extensive views across the plain as we descend steeply, with the villages 'sub Hamdon' dotted here and there. We reach the foot of the hill by an old mill with the wheel still in position, where we turn right and at the next junction go straight ahead for Chiselborough, thence following the signposts to Crewkerne (page 51).

From Crewkerne to Chard we overlap the previous route, with another opportunity to visit Forde Abbey, but if we have already done so we may prefer to drive straight to Chard on A30, on this stretch a fine high-set road. In Chard we turn right for Combe St Nicholas, where the routes diverge, for here we take the middle road where we have a choice of three ways, going forward over a subsequent wider road for Northay, then keeping right at the next fork. At the foot of a steep hill (bottom gear is advised) we go straight on for Bishopswood, crossing A303 on the way. Near the end of Bishopswood we bear left at a fork signposted Hemyock, in a mile crossing B3170 and descending into the Otter valley. We cross the infant stream near a dam and at the next major road, at the 'York' inn, turn right for Taunton. Thereafter we follow the Taunton signposts but at a crossroads 6½ miles from Wellington turn right towards Chard and at the 'Holman Clavel' inn left, again for Chard. At the next fork, where our way is once more signposted Taunton, we bear left.

We drive into Taunton (page 48), which we leave by the Minehead road, and at the Odeon cinema turn right towards the railway station, bearing left at the next traffic lights and after going under two railway bridges keep straight on, avoiding the Bridgwater turn. At a subsequent junction we go forward in the Minehead road, but where this turns left we go straight on and continue on this unsignposted road, steering towards the Quantock Hills and avoiding all side turnings. In just over two miles we come to the small village of Kingston, bearing left at its triangular green and right at the 'Swan' inn for Bridgwater.

When we reach the summit of this part of the Quantocks we bear half left for Aisholt past 'The Pines'. We continue on this hilly road, the rolling landscapes enlivened by the red soil of the ploughed fields and distant glimpses of the sea ahead in clear weather. We bear left at Courtway post office and after driving through a wooded glen emerge in sight of the fine stretch of water of the Hawkridge reservoir. Here we turn right for Bridgwater and after a long half mile turn hard right for Taunton, now bound for Quantock Forest. We keep left as far as a T-junction near the 'Travellers' Rest', where we turn left for Enmore along a ridge looking to the sea, then fork right up a narrow lane for North Petherton. We are now looking forward to Bridgwater, with Bridgwater Bay to our left.

We now drive straight over the forest ridge, following the next two signposts to North Petherton, but one and a half miles from Goathurst we fork right, avoid a later Goathurst turn, and at the next junction turn right into North Petherton, guided by its tall church tower. We bear left at a fork in the village for Bridgwater, then left at the main road but after a quarter of a mile leave it for a turning signposted Moorland on the right, at a later junction bearing right again, signposted Moorland and Burrow Bridge. We cross the Bridgwater and Taunton Canal and a railway and then come to the banks of the river Parrett, which we follow closely for almost a mile and a half, a pleasant interlude of contrast after the exciting hill country. When we leave the river we follow the signposts to Burrow Bridge over the willow-lined marshes and through the settlement of Moorland, rejoining the river bank at a T-junction and following it again towards Burrow Bridge.

We shall recognize Burrow Bridge by its conical hill, known as the Mump, crowned by a ruined church. This hill is believed to be the site of King Alfred's fort, occupied by him during his campaign against the Danes. Here we are driving through apple orchards, our road bordered by drains. We turn left over the bridge, passing the 'King Alfred' inn and driving under the Mump, and at the end of the marshes just after the road has climbed on to the drier ground of the island of Othery we turn right in sight of Othery church. We return to the marshes and at a junction just past a farm turn right along another willow-lined lane, which leads to Aller.

Aller, though showing little sign of antiquity, is famous as the place where the Danish leader, Guthrum, was baptized after his defeat by King Alfred at Ethandun. Here we turn right for Langport by an ancient tree in the centre of the village, and at a junction one mile short of Langport bear left for Pitney. At the next junction we turn left towards the Hams but at a right fork in about 200 yards resume the way to Pitney. We drive right through Pitney, a village of many thatched stone cottages grouped round the high-towered church, and on reaching a major road turn left in it.

This road takes us over Somerton Hill to Somerton, a fascinating town full of picturesque corners. The high ground on which it stands is the site of the former capital of the Sumersaetas, the Saxon tribe which gave Somerset its name. We pass some old gabled almshouses on the way to the centre, where there is a handsome octagonal market cross with gargoyles dating from the late seventeenth century, an impressive church with an unusual octagonal tower, and a Tudor market house with oriel windows. The 'Red Lion' inn still carries a notice 'licensed to let post horses', and there are many Tudor and Georgian houses in Broad Street and Coronation Street. Coming nearer to the present day, there is a fountain and trough commemorating the coronation of King Edward VII in 1902 in the little square with a central green.

We leave Somerton by the major road for Ilchester, which gives us good views to the outliers of the Mendip Hills, and continue on this B road, passing on our left the imposing Kingsdon Manor School just before crossing A372. We enter Ilchester past Northover church and drive into its centre, where there is a market cross with a sundial and weather vane similar to that at Martock (page 47). Just beyond the church, another with an octagonal tower, we turn left for Limington, where we go straight on for Ashington and the return to Yeovil.

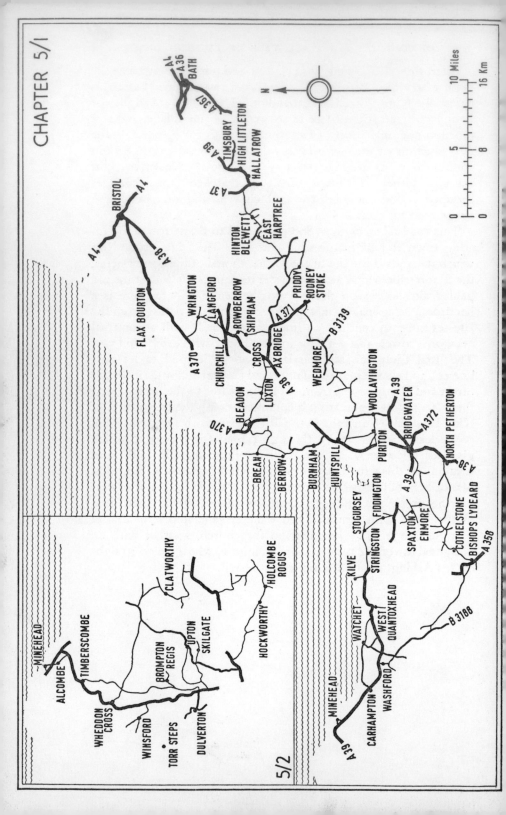

5/2

BRISTOL
A4
A38
FLAX BOURTON
A4
A370
WRINGTON
CHURCHILL
LANGFORD
ROWBERROW
SHIPHAM
CROSS
BLEADON
LOXTON
A38
AXBRIDGE
A371
PRIDDY
RODNEY STOKE
WEDMORE
B3139
A370
BREAN
BERROW
BURNHAM
HUNTSPILL
WOOLAVINGTON
PURITON
BRIDGWATER
A39
A372
NORTH PETHERTON
A38
STOGURSEY
FIDDINGTON
KILVE
STRINGSTON
SPAXTON
ENMORE
COTHELSTONE
BISHOPS LYDEARD
A358
WATCHET
WEST QUANTOXHEAD
B3188
MINEHEAD
CARHAMPTON
WASHFORD
A39

A4
A36
BATH
A367
A39
TIMSBURY
HIGH LITTLETON
HALLATROW
A37
HINTON BLEWETT
EAST HARPTREE

N

0   5   10 Miles
0   8   16 Km

MINEHEAD
ALCOMBE
TIMBERSCOMBE
CLATWORTHY
WHEDDON CROSS
BROMPTON REGIS
UPTON
SKILGATE
WINSFORD
TORR STEPS
DULVERTON
HOCKWORTHY
HOLCOMBE ROGUS

The fifteenth-century George Hotel, formerly a guest-house for pilgrims to Glastonbury Abbey. (Chapter 4.)

Sherborne Alms-houses, founded in 1437. (Chapter 4.)

The village of Low Ham, Somerset, under the Ham Hills.   (Chapter 4.)

The ancient clergy house, Muchelney.   (Chapter 4.)

CHAPTER FIVE

EXMOOR TO THE QUANTOCK HILLS

THE MAIN HILL COUNTRY of Somerset lies to the north parallel with the coast, where from east to west the Quantock Hills, the Brendon Hills and Exmoor cross the county, Exmoor extending into Devonshire. These hills all rise to well over 1,000 ft and Dunkery Beacon, the highest point of Exmoor, reaches a height of 1,707 ft above sea-level. The grand scenery of this part of Somerset is most conveniently explored from the popular holiday town of Minehead and the smaller coastal resorts nearby. One long tour is, however, included which starts from Bristol and Bath and crosses the Quantocks to Minehead, returning over the Mendips. Although it is well over 150 miles in length, it is comfortably within the compass of a long day's tour, particularly as its attractions are largely scenic.

We shall begin with this longer tour, leaving Bristol by the Clifton suspension bridge and after crossing the bridge keep right at the first junction, and right again at the entrance to Ashton Park (alternatively we can drive through the park, as on another route) on the Clevedon road, then take the first turning on the left alongside the park wall, which is again signposted Clevedon. At the end of the park we cross a major road for Flax Bourton, going over the wooded Ashton Hill with a long view forward to Dundry Hill, marked by Dundry church on its summit. We cross another major road just before entering Flax Bourton and in the village turn right for Weston, passing the church, its fine Norman south doorway visible from the road.

The next place we come to is Backwell West Town (Backwell proper lies to the left of our road) and a mile beyond this we turn left at a crossroads for Brockley Combe, a grand thickly wooded gash through the high rocks, which rise in precipitous cliffs above our road here and there. It is over a mile before we come out into open country again and we continue for another

mile, then turn right into a narrow lane opposite Downside post
box by a group of houses. This is a lovely road with splendid sea
and Mendip views, the main ridge appearing as a huge barrier
across our way.

At the next junction we bear right for Wrington and continue
to this village, guided by its glorious church tower, one of the
finest in a county noted for its exquisite church towers. We pass
the church and have the opportunity to see the rich tracery and
graceful pinnacles of the tower. The village itself is mainly
Georgian and we thread our way through its streets of handsome
houses on the Bridgwater road. At Langford we turn right at
the T-junction by the post office and in half a mile go forward into
the major road for Bridgwater, going forward again at the main
crossroads in Churchill. We drive through another wooded
gorge and after half a mile turn left for Rowberrow. On our left
the entrenchments of the prehistoric fort of Dolbury are a
prominent landmark, under the slopes of which stands the little
church of Rowberrow. Shortly after leaving Rowberrow we
enter the pretty village of Shipham and take the Cheddar road
past the modern church. This takes us into the gorge under
Callow Hill and Callow Rocks, unfortunately being extensively
quarried, then through the Perch, mercifully wooded, and emerge
in sight of the great round basin, usually gay with sailing boats,
that lies between Axbridge and Cheddar.

At the ensuing T-junction we turn right for Axbridge (page 20)
where we go forward through the square and the narrow High
Street, forking left for Bridgwater at the end of the town, following the southern flank of the Mendips. We cross the next main
road, A38, for Cross, which lies on the other side of the road,
and then go on for Loxton. Above us as we approach Loxton is a
little singular peak known as Crook Peak, a rock outcrop reaching
628 ft on the westerly spur of the Mendips which is continued in
Bleadon Hill. Loxton is seen across fields as a most attractive
composition of church and red-roofed cottages under Loxton
Hill, which faces Crook Peak on its east side.

From Loxton we continue to Bleadon, under the slopes of
Bleadon Hill, with the Axe valley on our left and occasional
glimpses of the winding river. At Bleadon village we can look
ahead to the sea, and just beyond the church we turn left on the
way signposted Weston, which brings us to A370. We cross

this right-handed by the 'Anchor' inn for Brean, the rocky
Brean Down to our right pointing a long finger across the Bristol
Channel. We drive over Bleadon Level, crossing the railway,
then running parallel with it, to the crossing of the Axe, shortly
afterwards recrossing the railway. At the next junction we turn
right for Brean and Burnham, and have to cross the railway yet
again then go forward on the other side for Brean. The landscape
is characteristic of the levels—fertile pastoral marshes divided
into fields by trees, tree-lined roads and reed-fringed drains.

At the next junction we turn left for Burnham and keep
straight on to Burnham via Berrow, where there is a tall lighthouse on the beach, with Brent Knoll, crowned by a hill fort,
prominent on our left. In Burnham we turn right by the fountain
on to the promenade and drive along it beside a fine sandy beach,
where there is another lighthouse. The church of St Andrew to
the left of the promenade has a Perpendicular tower which leans
slightly; inside there is an interesting reredos of white marble
with angels and cherubs in relief, which together with other
surviving fragments once formed an altar-piece designed for
Whitehall Chapel by Grinling Gibbons.

At the end of the promenade we turn left to the highroad and
right in it for Highbridge, there turning right on A38 for
Bridgwater and crossing the river Brue at the end of the town.
The next village is West Huntspill, at the end of which we turn
left for East Huntspill then right in a quarter of a mile beside a
house, shortly crossing the wide canalized Huntspill river. This
road takes us into Puriton, where we bear right past the church
and forward at the crossroads by the entrance arch to the manor-
house and right in a few yards for Glastonbury, and shortly left
down Puriton Hill to a T-junction, where we turn right across a
drain, and soon enter the outskirts of Bridgwater.

Bridgwater was formerly an important port on the tidal reach
of the river Parrett and a manufacturing centre. Although an
ancient town, it retains few medieval buildings, apart from the
parish church of St Mary, identified by its tall spire. A statue of
Admiral Blake, who was born in the town, stands in front of the
classical town hall. We leave Bridgwater by the Minehead road,
A39, then in about a quarter of a mile bear left in West Street for
Spaxton. At a junction just short of a large reservoir we turn left
and beyond the saddleback-towered church of Durleigh turn

right for Enmore. At Enmore a right turn at the 'Tynte Arms' leads to the church and manor-house. Two interesting features of the church are the quaint pinnacled stair turret on the handsome tower and the broken churchyard cross, while there is a glimpse of the house up the drive of Enmore Park just beyond the church.

The road past the church rejoins our direct road, in which we turn right to continue on our way, and at the next junction turn right again for Spaxton, which we reach by a series of delightful fern-banked lanes. At the first T-junction in this large village we turn right, then left in a quarter of a mile towards the church, which has a complete and well-preserved churchyard cross, and inside some fine carving, including massive carved wooden candelabras and bench ends. There is also a fine medieval tomb with figures looking as perfect as though they had been newly carved. We continue past the church and at the next junction turn left for Nether Stowey, then right at the next two junctions for Fiddington. This brings us to a main road at a post box, where right (care is necessary as we turn into this main road) but in about 200 yards turn left for Whitnell along a single-track lane, bearing left on reaching a broader road, which takes us into Fiddington. From there we follow the signposts to Stogursey, keeping right at one unsignposted fork.

Stogursey is a village of exceptional charm, its main street lined by trim cottages, some thatched, and handsome Georgian houses, with the base of the medieval cross and three fine chestnut trees in its centre. The priory church of St Andrew is a spacious one with a fine series of Norman arches and piers with carved capitals. The massive tub font is also Norman. The fine timber angel roof is of later date. All that remains of the priory buildings is a circular dovecot in the farmyard near the church. We leave Stogursey by turning left up the village street (away from the church), and beyond the village take the second turning on the left, signposted Stringston. Stringston church has a picturesque broach spire of red tiles and in the churchyard is a fine fourteenth-century cross with interesting carvings on the head.

We continue past the church (the entrance is just off our road), looking across to the Quantock Hills on our left, and at the next crossroads turn left for Williton then right at the subsequent major road for Minehead. This fine road crosses a shoulder of the Quantocks and we soon have a sea view all the way on our right.

We go through the villages of Kilve and West Quantoxhead, then fork right for Watchet, thence going on to Blue Anchor and Minehead (page 64).

We leave Minehead by the Bridgwater road, passing the watch tower of Dunster Castle high on its wooded hill and just beyond have the finest view of the castle, which looks most impressive standing clear of the trees on its lofty eminence. The tower of the church below rising just above the trees is the only sign of the village from this viewpoint. At the end of the park we enter the outskirts of Carhampton, where it is worth going into the church to see its magnificent rood screen. Not everyone approves of the modern repainting of the screen but at least it effectively brings out the detail of the carving. The much worn steps of the old cross stand in the churchyard.

Next we go on to Washford to visit Cleeve Abbey, for which we turn right in the dip just before the Washford river. Cleeve Abbey is unique in that most of the conventual buildings are remarkably complete, while only the foundations of the church remain. Even some of the wall paintings have survived to the present day. The abbey is open to the public daily throughout the year (afternoon only on Sunday) and should on no account be missed.

We go on past the abbey as far as the 'White Horse' inn, then left for Monksilver. After crossing a crossroads and passing a turning on the left, following the Monksilver signposts, we look for a small turning on the right signposted Nettlecombe Court. We follow this delightful little road (the thirteenth-century church and the Court are to the right), with occasional distant sea views between the high banks of beech and other hedgerow trees, for about three miles then turn left at a T-junction along the summit ridge of the Brendon Hills. At the next junction our way is signposted Taunton and we soon begin to descend and enjoy stupendous views ahead to the Quantocks and half right across the Vale of Taunton Deane to the Blackdown Hills.

We go forward over B3188, our way here signposted Taunton, but later signposted Bishop's Lydeard, to which we continue on this wider road, turning right into it on reaching the main road, A358, but take the first turning on the left, signposted Bridgwater, to go into the village. The church has a beautiful pinnacled 'Somerset' tower with pierced belfry windows. Inside, the fine fan-vaulted screen, which is coloured, the bench ends on which the various subjects are accented by coloured backgrounds and the Jacobean pulpit are well worth seeing by all who are interested in the ancient craft of woodcarving. For good measure in the churchyard there is a fourteenth-century cross with the figure of St John the Baptist carved on the shaft and reliefs on the base, also the steps and shaft of the former village cross.

We now turn into the High Street, passing the medieval almshouses, which happily are well restored, on our right and continue on the Bridgwater road. After just over a mile we see the manorial group of the Jacobean house and medieval church of Cothelstone through the entrance arch, which was the scene of one of the many cruel deeds of the notorious Judge Jeffreys, who ordered two of Monmouth's followers at the time of the abortive rebellion to be hanged from it. The quaint detached gatehouse in front of the house is really a lodge.

We now begin to climb the wooded slopes of Cothelstone Hill, with a bird's-eye view of the group and also of the later square classical Cothelstone House. Cothelstone was an ancient Beacon hill and has a round tower on its summit. There is a large car park near the highest point of the road, from whence it is only a short walk to the tower. There are fine views to the Brendon Hills, the Quantocks, and to the Mendips and the sea. We descend from the Beacon as far as a right turn for North Petherton, which we take, proceeding along the razor-like edge of a hill with long views on both sides. We keep right at the next T-junction and at the Broomfield turn, then follow the signposts to North Petherton. We turn left into the village but immediately turn right in Tappers Lane to the main road, where left past the church, which has a magnificent tower, beautifully ornamented with pierced windows and pinnacles, another contender for the description 'finest of the Somerset towers'.

We go on from here to Bridgwater and at the Ring Road turn right for Glastonbury then shortly fork right at the 'Cross Rifles' inn on A39, signposted Bath. After crossing the King's Sedge-moor Drain we follow the main road for another quarter of a mile then turn left by the 'Knowle' inn over the modest eminence of Knowle Hill, in less than a mile coming to the next village of Woolavington. In sight of its church we turn right to the major road, then left in this for Bason Bridge. Half a mile beyond the crossing of the wide Huntspill canalized river we turn right, and at the next junction turn left for Edington Burtle and continue towards this little village over level moors divided by hedges and drains and backed by the line of the Mendips. We cross the Cripps river by a narrow hump-backed bridge, then a level crossing, and finally the river Brue by an old stone bridge, our way here signposted Wedmore, towards which we turn right in about 200 yards. We continue along the willow-lined roads, turning right, then left, and on reaching a hamlet turn right along the edge of the moor to a T-junction, where left, thence continuing to Wedmore (keeping right at one unsignposted junction). This sounds complicated, but is fairly obvious in practice, as the roads must follow the lines of the many drains and dykes and lead to the bridges crossing them.

We turn right into Wedmore, then left, following the Cheddar road past the fine parish church and the 'George' inn. The village shows little sign, however, of the antiquity that might be expected of a place where the famous Treaty of Wedmore was concluded in 879 between King Alfred and the Danes after he had defeated them at Ethandun. A mile beyond the outskirts we turn right for Draycott, bearing right again in 200 yards, then right once again on the other side of the river Axe, signposted Rodney Stoke.

Rodney Stoke lies at the foot of the Mendips, here looking green and fertile, the cultivated fields reaching high up the slopes towards the summit. We turn right at a junction as we approach the village, then right again just beyond the pleasant little church, and on to a major road, which we cross and climb the steep hill to the summit of the Mendips. Here we have extensive views to Glastonbury Tor in the south, and to Brent Knoll and the sea retrospectively, and just off the road are a number of Round Barrows and a notable Long Barrow (prehistoric burial mounds).

Just beyond the summit of the hill we turn right into an obscure unsignposted road (in sight of a distant village to the right). This road takes us to Priddy, a lead-mining centre from Roman times, and at its large triangular green we bear left and at the top of the village right in Nine Barrows Lane, which passes near two groups of barrows, the Priddy Nine Barrows and Ashen Hill Barrows. At the ensuing T-junction we turn right on a broader road and continue to a crossroads, where we turn left towards Burrington Combe, leaving this major road at 'Castle of Comfort' inn for a sharp right turn to East Harptree. Soon the shining waters of the vast Chew Valley Lake are ahead of us as we descend into East Harptree, crossing several crossroads on the outskirts and in the village, at the other end going on for Widcombe, where we neglect the Litton turn on the right but take a right turn fifty yards farther, currently unsignposted, a pretty road which takes us uphill again for another fine view into the Chew valley and to distant Blagdon Lake beyond and to the left of the Chew Valley Lake.

At a junction by a house we bear left, and left again to the church of Hinton Blewett, then bear left yet once more before turning right for Cameley, passing its church, almost solitary and noteworthy only for its Perpendicular red sandstone tower. At the next main road, which is the A37 to Bristol (only a dozen miles away), we cross right-handed for a road signposted to a variety of government establishments, and after going under a railway bridge we turn right immediately for Hallatrow, which lies on the main road A39, and where Bath is only ten miles away to the left. A pleasant alternative return to Bath is to turn right in about three-quarters of a mile in High Littleton just past the church, signposted Timsbury, and proceed to this high-set village built along a shelf overlooking the Cam valley. At its end we bear right into the Bath road and quickly reach the outskirts of the city.

The remaining tours in this chapter are routed from Minehead, an attractive town protected by the bold North Hill which shelters its harbour and strand. Minehead is really three towns in one—the original fishing settlement beside the harbour, where stands the tiny fishermen's chapel on the quay by the 'Pier' hotel; the 'old town' grouped round the medieval church on the steep slopes of North Hill and the modern holiday resort with its handsome promenade and many hotels and guest houses.

It is well worth climbing the steep steps to see the parish church of St Michael, guided by its conspicuous Perpendicular tower, and the many picturesque corners of the old town, which has many charming houses and cottages, and, not least, to admire the magnificent views from the churchyard. Inside the church the splendid rood screen and the interesting font are among many features worth seeing.

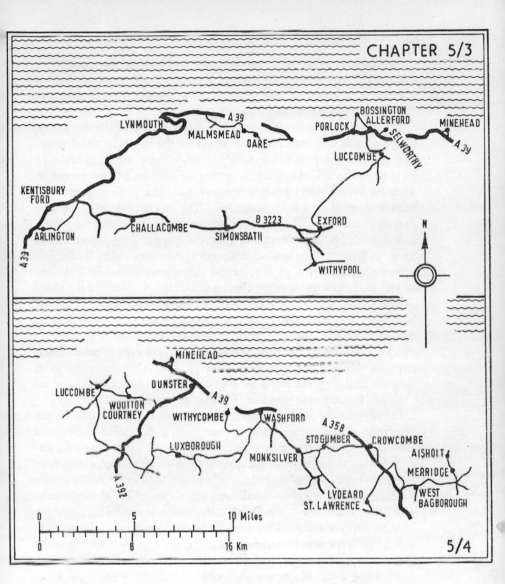

In the later town, in Wellington Square, a new church has been built, to the outside of which has been transferred the statue of Queen Anne which formerly graced the parish church, and in the market place and main street are the former assembly rooms next to the modern market hall, and opposite these is an ancient building which was once the court house. In Market House Lane, which runs by the side of the market hall, a row of

65

almshouses built in 1630 survives, in front of which stands the shaft and base of the old market cross. A whole morning, or afternoon, is scarcely long enough to set aside for exploring in detail this fascinating three-in-one town.

The first tour from Minehead, covering just under 90 miles, starts on the Dunster road but at Alcombe we take the byroad just beyond the post office to Dunster, a very pretty alternative to the main road. Dunster is justly famous, an artist's paradise, with its broad street leading the eye past the ancient octagonal yarn market to the castle on the hill. The street is lined by mellow gabled houses, notably the 'Luttrell Arms' with a medieval porch, and it is dominated on the north by Conygar Hill, surmounted by a 'gazebo' watch tower. For good measure there is the fine priory church with a glorious rood screen, the dovecot and barn of the early priory nearby; the curious old building with three overhanging storeys and Gothic windows and known as the Nunnery, may also have links with the priory. Dunster Castle, the home of the Luttrell family since the fourteenth century, is open to visitors in the summer months (Wednesdays and Thursdays in June, Tuesdays, Wednesdays and Thursdays in July, August and September, and Bank Holiday Mondays). From October to May it is open on Wednesday afternoons.

Finally, as we leave Dunster by the main road south in the direction of the castle, Park Street on the left leads to the old Gallox Bridge, a stone packhorse bridge of two arches (the car park is just short of it). We now follow A396 towards Tiverton as far as Timberscombe church, where we turn left for Brompton Regis, climbing steeply uphill and after two miles along a fern-lined lane reach the 1,000-ft contour, looking across to Dunkery Beacon on our right. Our way at first is signposted Dulverton but when we come to a signposted crossroads we turn right for Wheddon Cross, then left in about 200 yards for Winsford, descending into the wooded Quarme valley, where we cross A396 right-handed, i.e. right then left in 100 yards up a steep hill, with an even more steep descent into Winsford, going forward at the foot in a wider road and crossing the river Exe beside an old packhorse bridge, used as a footbridge since the road was built. In the attractive village centre by the ford over the Exe, the thatched cottages dominated by the high-set church standing sentinel above, we bear left past the 'Royal Oak' for Tarr Steps.

We climb over a shoulder of Winsford Hill to reach Tarr Steps, going forward at a crossroads in the middle of the moor, bearing left over a cattle grid, and soon come to the famous steps, a picturesque footbridge of enormous stone slabs, believed to be of prehistoric origin. The ford here can be rather deep so it is safer to retrace our way briefly, then turn right for Dulverton. This time we continue into Dulverton, at first looking across to Dartmoor in the south, later descending to the wooded glen of the river Barle which we follow into the town.

In the centre of Dulverton we cross the square, keeping the church on our left, and continue on the road signposted Minehead, shortly crossing the Exe. Here we turn left just beyond the bridge to take in part of the Exe gorge, alongside the wild animal sanctuary of Barlynch Wood on our right. After driving along a fine three-mile stretch beside the Exe we turn right by a white house for Brompton Regis, continuing over a crossroads at the top of the hill and bearing left at a T-junction. Just beyond the inn and church at Brompton Regis we bear right, then left in a quarter of a mile, for Watchet.

After going over a green hill and crossing a little stream we turn right at the next three junctions, all signposted Upton. This brings us to a T junction in Upton, where we turn right for about 200 yards, then left for Skilgate, climbing to the summit of Haddon Hill and down steeply into Skilgate, there bearing right past the church, rebuilt in late Victorian times, and drive along the valley. We go straight on at a crossroads where Raddington is signposted and thence follow the wooded valley of the Batherm, keeping right at two junctions and then re-crossing the river.

At the next T-junction we turn left for Bampton, shortly crossing a major road for Clayhanger. At the crossroads just short of the village, however, we turn right for Hockworthy, to which we follow the signposts, at the outskirts forking right into the village centre down a steep hill. We continue down this hill beyond the village and bear left for Holcombe Rogus. On the way we pass the lovely park of Holcombe Court, a magnificent early Tudor mansion, which is open on Bank Holiday afternoons and on other days by arrangement. The nearby church is also interesting, built chiefly in the Perpendicular style, with a tall tower, and contains monuments of the Bluett family, who owned Holcombe Court until last century.

We continue through the village on the Wellington road past
the Court and church, but where Greenham is signposted to the
left we leave the Wellington road and make for Greenham, turn
ing right for Cothay at Greenham Barton, an imposing Tudor
manor-house which retains a medieval Gothic gatehouse. The
signposts soon bring us to Cothay manor-house, which has been
described as 'the most perfect surviving fifteenth-century country
house'. Situated near the bank of the river Tone, it has a great
hall and minstrels gallery, and a gatehouse converted into a chapel.
It is well worth a visit and is open on Wednesday and Thursday
afternoons from mid-May to mid-September, also the first
Sunday in the month from June to September and Bank Holiday
Sundays and Mondays (not Easter).

From there we go on for Langford Budville and at a junction
two miles short of Wellington, in sight of the red roofs of the
town backed by the Blackdown Hills, we turn left for Wivelis-
combe. In this little main road town we bear left in sight of the
church and left again in High Street, then right at the 'White
Hart' inn for Langley Marsh just after passing a quaint tiled
building with elaborate wood carving. At a T-junction in Langley
we turn left for Clatworthy, in less than a quarter of a mile right,
and right again at the next junction, for Raleigh's Cross. We are
now climbing gradually over the Brendon Hills, with splendid
views to the left over the Vale of Taunton Deane to the Blackdown Hills.

At a crossroads a signpost shows the way to 'Reservoir
Viewing Site' and this road is well worth following through
Clatworthy to see a fine piece of engineering in the high dam,
and the lovely expanse of Clatworthy reservoir (entrance through
gates), tranquil in its wooded shores. We must return to
Clatworthy village and thence back to the junction and turn left
to resume our way to Raleigh's Cross, turning left to it at a
T-junction at the summit of the hills. At the 'Ralegh's Cross' (note
different spelling here!) we continue for Wheddon Cross, with
the sea to our right and Exmoor ahead. We fork right for
Wheddon Cross after half a mile, our road exceeding 1,300 ft
with glorious views on every hand as we continue for Wheddon
Cross. There we turn right for Minehead along an attractive
wooded shelf road and so drive back, rejoining our outward way
at Timberscombe.

Our next tour from Minehead takes us into the heart of Exmoor and across the Devon boundary to make our exploration of its romantic and sometimes wild scenery more complete. Like the previous tour, it covers a distance of roughly 90 miles. We leave Minehead by the Porlock road, soon entering the Exmoor National Park. The first signposted turn, though quite passable, is described as unsuitable for cars, which owing to its narrowness is probably true in the busy season. However, the main road is a most attractive one with fine Exmoor views, so we lose little by taking it as far as the next signposted turn for Selworthy at Holnicote. Selworthy, which lies under Selworthy Beacon (1,013 ft), is a deservedly popular village, now in the care of the National Trust. Its thatched cottages with the typical Exmoor round chimneys clustered round the green and nestling here and there among the trees make a perfect composition. The church of All Saints in the Perpendicular style stands high above the village looking out over Porlock Vale to Dunkery Beacon. The church, unusual in lying south-east to north-west because of the lie of the land, has exceptionally fine waggon roofs, especially that of the south aisle, which is beautifully painted. There is an interesting pew over the porch, reached from the chamber above the porch, and the circular bowl font is Norman. A short distance from the church is a fine buttressed tithe barn dating from the fourteenth century. You will not feel that an hour or two spent in exploring this charming village has been wasted.

Now we return to the main road and continue to Allerford, there turning right for Bossington, which takes us past the wonderfully preserved packhorse bridge, a graceful composition of two stone arches. At Bossington, another charming village under Bossington Hill, from which a road leads to a beach on Porlock Bay, we bear left in the centre for Porlock and continue downhill to Porlock church. The town is now separated from the sea and its beach and harbour are at Porlock Weir a mile and a half to the north-west. There are several interesting old houses and cottages in the town near the church, the exterior of which is less interesting than the interior, where several notable tombs are to be found.

From the church we return briefly on our tracks and turn hard round at a hairpin bend towards Minehead, subsequently turning right where Luccombe is signposted. After passing West

Luccombe, noting another picturesque packhorse bridge, we continue to a signposted crossroads (short of Luccombe village) where we turn right steeply uphill for Dunkery Beacon. At the next fork, however, we leave the Dunkery road, bearing right for Exford. This road takes us higher than the Dunkery road and reaches over 1,550 ft at its highest point, first going steeply down a wooded glen to cross the East Water by a ford. The views are splendid as we climb up towards the Beacon and we reach a point only 150 ft lower than its 1,707 ft which makes it the highest summit on Exmoor. A ridge path leads to the top over the gorse, heather and whortleberry.

The descent is very gradual to Exford Common, which we go over into Exford, a pleasant village round a green. We leave it by the Withypool road, crossing the river Exe, and at the next crossroads turn left on the Dulverton road for less than a quarter of a mile, leaving it by a right fork. This takes us straight into Withypool, where we turn right at the 'Royal Oak' inn, pass the church and cross the old bridge of six arches over the river Barle, turning right for South Molton on the other side. We drive over the gorse-clad Withypool Common, with the green Withypool Hill rising to 1,306 ft on our left.

We proceed towards the Moltons to just beyond the 'Sportsman's Inn', where we turn right for Simonsbath over Exmoor Forest along a road which forms the county boundary with Devon, into which we have fine views off the edge of the forest as far as distant Dartmoor on a clear day. After over three miles or so on the exhilarating high ridge we come to a crossroads where we turn right for Simonsbath, and continue on this road to Simonsbath. We pass a large cairn to John William Fortescue, historian of the British Army, and soon look down into the valley of the upper Barle as we approach the village in its wooded combe, where left on the other side of the river, and left again in a few yards, for Challacombe. We reach this scattered village a mile or so over the Devon border and there continue towards Blackmoor Gate, turning right at the next major road.

We pass the Wistland Pound reservoir in its attractive setting on our left, then turn left for Loxhore, a quarter of a mile short of A39, which is usually within earshot if not within sight! We follow this typical beech-hedged and fern-banked Devon lane for about two miles, then take the second turning on the right, signposted Arlington. At a T-junction at the foot of this lane we bear right, away from Arlington Church road. This takes us past Arlington Court, a fascinating National Trust property open to the public every day except Saturday from April to September. This former manor-house of the Chichester family, rebuilt in the Regency period, well repays a visit, not only to see the house and furniture but also the interesting collections of shells and model ships, in addition to numerous *objets d'art*.

Our way now continues past the house as far as the main road, in which we turn right and follow as far as Kentisbury Ford, where we leave it, going straight on for Combe Martin. When we reach the main Combe Martin road, A399, we turn right for Blackmoor Gate and in a quarter of a mile left for 'Hunter's Inn', enjoying splendid views across the heather moors to the sea. We descend through thick hanging woods to the bank of a tributary of the river Heddon, crossing it, and also the Heddon, at 'Hunter's Inn'. After passing the inn we ascend the valley, a romantic drive through the ferny glen with the stream of the Heddon chattering along beside us. There are one or two sharp corners on this narrow road which need a little care.

Eventually we come to the main Lynmouth road and turn left towards this famous resort. The best approach to it is to fork right short of Lynton, which takes us high above the lovely wooded gorge of the West Lyn and then down to the East Lyn, turning left at the Watersmeet signpost, where there is an ample car park. This is considered by many to be one of the most impressive drives in the west country. We leave Lynmouth by Countisbury Hill (Porlock and Minehead road), which, although it has a gradient of 1 in 5 and seems very steep as we begin the climb, holds no terrors. As one might expect, the views are magnificent from the top, where we turn right for Brendon, there crossing the river and bearing left for Oare.

At Malmsmead we find the Lorna Doone Farm, and nearby the hotel, gift shop and tea garden, basking in the borrowed fame of being the scene of R. D. Blackmore's *Lorna Doone*. On payment of a small fee one can walk along a footpath from here to the Doone valley. Where Oare Water joins Badgworthy Water we turn left over the bridge for Oare, riding high above the river as the road follows the Oare valley. Soon we pass Oare church where Lorna Doone was shot down at her wedding, and there is a

memorial to R. D. Blackmore. Our road goes on to Robbers
Bridge and Oareford, still following the course of the Oare
Water, then crossing it by the narrow bridge, which is only seven
feet wide. We go up a 1 in 4 hill at one point, with a magnificent view into the deep cleft of the Weir Water valley, soon
after this bearing right into the main road on the top of the moor.
    It only remains now to drive back to Minehead via Porlock,
but the fine sea and cliff views to our left make this main road a
memorable one. At its highest point it attains 1,143 ft, giving
immense vistas in every direction. There is ample accommodation
for cars to draw off to admire the view and for picnics.
    Our final tour from Minehead takes us from Exmoor over the
Brendon and the Quantock Hills. It is a rather shorter tour of
about 80 miles and, as its features are principally scenic, suitable
for a long afternoon's drive, perhaps with a stop for tea. We
again leave Minehead by the Dunster road and continue through
Dunster on the Tiverton road. At a bridge over the Avill river
after half a mile we fork right into a wooded lane, currently
unsignposted, an exceptionally pretty lane with high fern-clad
banks which later comes out into open fields and eventually
brings us to the village of Wootton Courtney. This is a compact
little settlement grouped under its saddle-back-towered church,
where we go on for Luccombe, another pretty village of thatched
cottages grouped round a handsome church, just beyond which
we bear left for Dunkery Beacon, and left again at a subsequent
crossroads, climbing up through woods to the bare slopes of the
Beacon. There are grand views from this road, into the combes
on our right, along the coast to the left, and to the Brendon Hills
and Quantocks lying near the coast, and we pass the cairn on the
Beacon quite closely (a footpath leads to it) then descend gently.
    At the signpost at the foot of Dunkery Beacon we go forward
for Wheddon Cross and at the 'Rest and Be Thankful' inn we go
forward at the crossing for Brendon Hill. At the next crossroads
we turn left for Luxborough, and right at the next two junctions
for the same village. We keep right once more at Luxborough's
church, another with a saddle-back tower, and beyond it turn
left, then right, i.e. following the road steeply downhill to a
T-junction, where left for Roadwater, but soon fork left again
for Withycombe, climbing up to a shelf in dense woods, with
the Brendon Hills to the right.

Greenham Barton manor-house, showing the fine medieval gatehouse. (Chapter 5.)

The entrance to Cothelstone, where two of Monmouth's followers were hanged by order of Judge Jeffreys. (Chapter 5.)

Tarr Steps, an ancient bridge over the Barle believed to date from prehistoric times. (Chapter 5.)

The well-preserved gatehouse of Cleeve Abbey. (Chapter 5.)

We descend to a little cluster of houses in a combe and thence on to Withycombe, another pleasant village round a sturdy-towered little church, and from there go forward for Carhampton, turning right on reaching the main road for Washford. In Washford we turn right alongside the Washford river for Cleeve Abbey (see page 61) and soon after passing the entrance go forward for Monksilver, continuing to it along a pretty valley road leading towards the Quantocks. We bear right into the village and at its end turn left up a steep tunnel of trees for Stogumber, keeping left at each subsequent junction until we come to this large and distinguished village. Here we turn right for Crowcombe, passing the fine Perpendicular church with a commanding tower on our left.

We now begin our climb into the Quantocks as we near Crowcombe, our way along fern-banked lanes. Crowcombe is an interesting village, which we enter past the 'Carew Arms' and a fine village cross. There is a thirteenth-century cross with sculptured figures beside an old yew in the churchyard and opposite the church the ruins of a pre-Reformation building which formerly served as an almshouse and school. Crowcombe Court, beside the church, is a good red-brick classical mansion.

Just beyond the church we turn left for Nether Stowey up another wooded hill with luxuriant ferns beside the road, then across the ridge, which commands splendid views. We fork right at the summit and follow the signposts down to Nether Stowey, going through the outskirts to the main road, Lime Street, lined with handsome houses. The poet Coleridge's gracious Georgian cottage, open daily except Saturdays from March to October, is on the right opposite the 'First and Last' inn. The quaint summer-house abutting on the road belongs to Stowey Court, a fifteenth-century mansion beside the church.

We return to Castle Street (only the foundations and ramparts of the castle survive) where we turn left for Over Stowey and left in South Lane, where Taunton is signposted, and across the next crossroads. After another mile we leave the Taunton road for a right turn to Cockercombe and Triscombe Stone. The combe is a very pretty one beside which we proceed through a rhododendron-lined drive for much of the way, bearing left with the surfaced road at the summit. The Triscombe Stone is on the Roman road and only a rough track continues. There are,

however, rewarding views and a parking place. We must return
to the junction and there turn right for Taunton, but at the
subsequent junction, 8½ miles from Taunton, we turn away from
it on the Aisholt road to the right, bearing right again at the next
junction. We turn left at the two next forks, which brings us into
Aisholt in its deep combe, passing the picturesque thatched old
School House by the stream.

Beyond the village we neglect the first right fork by a brick
cavern but in just over half a mile turn right by a house on the
hillside and after going through the hamlet of Lower Merridge
come to a major road (only 5 miles from Taunton) where we
turn right for Cothelstone. At the next junction we turn right
for West Bagborough and continue to this village, which lies
outside the park of Bagborough House. We drive beside the
park wall and at the junction at the end of the village turn left
for Minehead. On reaching a main road, A358, we turn right for
a quarter of a mile, then left for Lydeard St Lawrence, in a short
half mile turning right downhill in a narrower road. We turn
right again into the village and pass the fine church with its
handsome pinnacled tower. Near the end of the village we turn
left for Westowe, and left again in that little hamlet, then left a
third time for Willett, going forward in a wider road for Raleigh's
Cross and driving towards the prominent tower on Willett Hill.

At 'Ralegh's Cross' inn we go forward for Wheddon Cross,
keeping right in half a mile and in another two miles fork right
for Luxborough, thence returning to Dunster and Minehead.

CHAPTER SIX

THE COTSWOLD

THE COTSWOLD is undoubtedly the best known and most popular (perhaps too popular at holiday times) scenic highlight of the West Country. The oolitic limestone of which the vast undulating plateau is composed gives its towns and villages a homogeneous appearance almost without parallel in England, for without exception they are built of this limestone, which weathers to a mellow golden hue in a very short time, so that even houses built recently harmonize with their older companions. For this reason it has been the policy of local councils to continue the use of Cotswold stone for new houses in spite of the fact that costs are much higher than they would be if brick or synthetic materials were used.

One of the best centres for exploring the Cotswold in detail is Cheltenham, which because it has been a spa town since Regency times has many hotels and guest houses of all grades. Gloucester, where there is also plenty of accommodation, lies only nine miles distant to the west, so that motorists from that city are almost equally well placed for the following tours.

Cheltenham lies under the extreme western edge of the Cotswold. The town was beautifully laid out in the Regency period, and its wide tree-lined boulevards and flower-filled gardens are a fitting background to the noble public buildings and pleasant domestic terraces. Among the many fine buildings, for the most part in the Georgian 'Grecian' style, are the Pump Room in Pittville Gardens, the municipal offices in the Promenade, the Montpellier Rotunda, and the town hall. The private houses are in various beautiful styles of the period, many with the typical lacy ironwork balconies and porches, while the shopping centre is one of the most handsome in England. An intriguing feature is the row of caryatids outside the shops in Montpellier Walk. Most of the churches, including the medieval parish church and

75

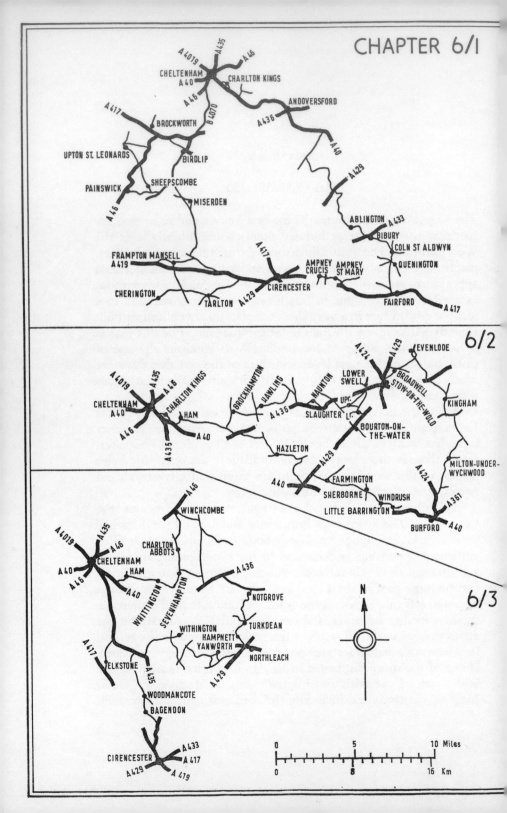

6/2

6/3

N

the Victorian ones, are in the Gothic style, as are the two famous colleges, Cheltenham College for boys, and the Ladies' College.

Our first tour, of about 85 miles, leaves Cheltenham by the Bath road, A46 (also signposted Stroud), passing Cheltenham College. Soon after that we fork left on B4070 for Birdlip, climbing steeply uphill and looking across to the Malverns on our right over the Vale of Severn. On the summit of Birdlip Hill it is worth stopping in the layby to admire the magnificent vistas to Gloucester and the Vale of Severn, to the Malvern Hills, and to the Forest of Dean beyond the Severn. We go on into the high-set Birdlip village, there turning right on the Stroud road and just beyond the 'Royal George' inn go straight down the steep slopes of Birdlip Hill through hanging woods, looking across to the large reservoir in Witcombe Park.

We bear left to pass the little Norman church with a later tower, noting the venerable spreading yew tree in the churchyard, then we follow the road to the right back to the wider road, in which we turn left and soon go forward in the Gloucester road. Just beyond this point we look for a sign to a Roman villa on the left, which is well worth visiting not only for its archaeological interest but also for the lovely ride to it, the road going south of the lake. The villa is still being excavated but most of the foundations and parts of the mosaic floors of the baths have been uncovered.

We return to the main road and continue to Brockworth, where we turn left on A46 for Stroud. (Gloucester motorists can join here via A417 if they wish to see the Roman villa, or later at Upton St Leonards.) We pass the foot of Cooper's Hill, the scene of the traditional cheese-rolling ceremony which takes place every Whit Monday, marked by a flagstaff. We skirt Gloucester, seen far to our right dominated by the graceful cathedral tower, turning sharp right for Upton St Leonards, at a fork turning right again into the village on the Gloucester road, then at a T-junction by a postbox turn left, again for Gloucester. At the subsequent T-junction we turn left away from Gloucester on the road signposted Cranham.

We pass the entrance to the modern Prinknash Abbey, rebuilt on the site of an ancient monastery. Visitors are welcomed to the abbey, where the monks have established a flourishing pottery industry, famous for its black lustre ware among other products.

We continue from there uphill, at the top bearing right for Painswick. Painswick Beacon, crowned by a prehistoric hill fort, rises on our right and a turning in just under a mile takes us to it and through its entrenchments to a point well over the 900-ft contour. There are parking places nearby so that we can enjoy the superb views at our leisure. We can continue from here on the same road, which makes a hairpin turn to the left on reaching a wider road which takes us into Painswick.

Painswick is one of my favourite Cotswold towns, a place full of charming corners, the houses of all periods but all of the local white freestone, forming a harmonious composition. In the centre of the town stands the spacious church, the magnificent tower and spire a landmark for miles around. Even more famous are the clipped yew trees in the churchyard, said to number ninety-nine and mostly dating from the end of the eighteenth century. The nearby Court House is a fine Elizabethan manor-house, and contains the original Court Room of King Charles I. It is open to the public on Thursday afternoons from the beginning of June until the end of September.

We return from the church to the traffic lights and at the crossroads beyond them turn right for Sheepscombe, bearing right down a steep hill where Sheepscombe is signposted again. We pass the splendid Loveday's Mill, which is partly Tudor, and at a fork by the Methodist church bear left down to the village, which has a quaint Regency church in the Early English and Decorated styles of Gothic, with a tiny dome crowning its slender pinnacled tower. By the church we turn sharp right uphill for Miserden, climbing through hanging woods and crossing the next two crossroads. We pass an old house called 'Wishanger', with an interesting porch and coat of arms, and a group of barns and farm buildings beside it. Soon after this we take a left fork into Miserden, a pretty village on the edge of Miserden (or Misarden) Park, the gardens of which are occasionally open to visitors during the summer.

At the next crossroads we bear left towards Cirencester, at a fork right for Sapperton, then go straight on at the next junction. At the foot of the hill by the 'Daneway' inn we cross the river Frome, then at a crossroads in just over a quarter of a mile we turn right for Frampton Mansell, going through this on the Chalford road. When we reach a major road we turn right in it towards Stroud but leave this road in less than a mile for the Minchinhampton turn on the left and continue on this for about two miles. Soon after passing a well-marked barrow, at 'Ragged Cot' inn we turn left for Avening, now looking forward over the wide plain watered by the infant Thames and its many tributaries. At a clump of beech trees we turn left for Cherington then right for Nag's Head, where we turn left and continue to Cherington.

We go through Cherington on the Cirencester road (two left turns) and continue to 'Lowesmoor' farm, where we turn right over a field road for Tarlton and go straight on into this village of pretty thatched cottages. There we take the Kemble turns, which bring us in a mile and a quarter to a main road, the Foss Way, in which we turn left to Cirencester. We pass the 'Thames Head' inn, then cross Thames Head bridge, on this ancient Roman road, pass the Gothic buildings of the Royal Agricultural College, and finally drive into the town alongside Cirencester Park. After exploring the town (see page 85), if we have not already done so, we leave it by A417 for Lechlade and follow this road as far as Ampney Crucis, where we turn left into the village and straight on past the stump of the village cross. The church is to the left of our road, just beyond the bridge over the Ampney brook. The church is an interesting one with Norman, and possibly Saxon, features, and in the churchyard is a fine cross, exceptionally well-preserved because its gabled head was hidden away for many years.

At a venerable elm on the tiny green in this pretty village we fork right for Ampney St Mary, also a pretty village, where we bear right at another little green triangle, this time with a single horse chestnut tree. At a T-junction beyond this village we turn left then cross the next crossroads for Quenington, but at the next junction, a five-way one, we bear half right for Fairford. At a T-junction we turn left for Lechlade, then into the stone-built village of Fairford, over the river Coln. We turn left again into the broad market place and through it for the church, famous internationally for its unique painted glass windows, dating from the end of the fifteenth century. The church is a fine one, with a handsome pinnacled tower and other interesting features, but the twenty-eight beautiful windows should on no account be missed.

At the next junction we turn left for Quenington alongside

Fairford Park and in two miles come to this picturesque village where we cross a lovely reach of the Coln by the mellow manor-house and pass the original gatehouse of a preceptory of Knights Hospitallers founded at the end of the twelfth century. The next village of Coln St Aldwyn is almost contiguous, and we veer off to the right at The Green to it, soon recrossing the river into its centre. The church and the Elizabethan manor-house are just to the left off the Bibury road, along which we proceed, with lovely views into the Coln valley as we drop down into Bibury. Bibury is probably the most admired of the many distinguished villages on the Coln. We catch a glimpse of the early Jacobean Bibury Court beside the church, which is an interesting one with several authenticated Saxon features, as we enter the village alongside the river. The picturesque stone bridges and charming gabled stone cottages, notably Arlington Row, and the 'Swan' hotel combine to make this one of the loveliest villages in England.

We go straight on past the 'Swan' with the river on our left, and in less than a mile reach the hamlet of Ablington, where we find another fine Elizabethan manor-house, distinguished by the heraldic beasts guarding the gate. We bear right just beyond this for Cheltenham, rising to the Wold, here comparatively bleak and treeless. We cross two crossroads, then on reaching the Foss Way, A429, cross it right-handed and continue towards Cheltenham, going by way of Andoversford and Charlton Kings. Gloucester motorists fork left for Seven Springs before reaching Andoversford, and thence by A436 and A417 back to Gloucester.

Our second tour, of about 75 miles, takes us across the Wold to the Oxfordshire border and visits several favourite villages and beauty spots. Gloucester motorists can join the tour by driving direct to Cheltenham on A40, by which road, the London and Oxford road, we leave the town centre of Cheltenham, and continue as far as Charlton Kings, where about a quarter of a mile beyond its sign we turn left in Ryeworth Road. We soon emerge into open country and continue in Ham Road, which takes us through Ham village, where we bear right uphill at the green near the end of the village. From this point we climb steadily up to the summit of the Wold, where the wide and attractive vistas cover 180 degrees of vision. We continue on this fine byway, neglecting one or two farm roads to the left, and at a junction go forward for Brockhampton past a charming group of Tudor cottages, keeping right, again for Brockhampton, at the next junction in about half a mile. Shortly after that, however, we leave the Brockhampton road and go straight on for Andoversford, leaving that road in turn, for we soon bear left and on reaching a main road (A436) turn left in it for a quarter of a mile. (This is a convenient place for motorists from Gloucester to join the route, coming via A417 and Seven Springs.)

Now we leave A436 for a right turn to Hazleton, driving over smiling and cultivated Wold country with only gentle undulations, the green of the fields broken up by the darker green hedges. At a T-junction after about two miles we turn right, again signposted Hazleton, and fork left at the next junction past two clearly discernible long barrows on the left of the road. The next left turn takes us into Hazleton village past the church, clearly one of Norman foundation with a fine chancel arch and south doorway and a single round-headed east window of that period. At the church we bear right through the village, then left at the next junction but turn right almost immediately down an obscure narrow road, which is unsignposted. We follow this peaceful road until in about a mile and a half it becomes a grassy track at a junction, where we turn left. After passing a fine manor farm our road bears right under a wooded hill, under which is an attractive house seen from our road across a little stream.

We go straight on past the Turkdean turn for Farmington, to which the signposts lead us, crossing A429 *en route*. At Farmington's green, recognized by its quaint gabled shelter, formerly a pump or well canopy, we bear right past the church and the four-square manor-house, facing each other across the road. Thence we continue to Sherborne, following the course of the winding Sherborne Brook, which joins the Windrush beyond Sherborne village. As we go over a crossroads we reach the wall of Sherborne Park, which became the King's School for Boys. As well as admiring the many magnificent mature trees in the park on our right, we catch a glimpse of the church, house and stable block. The village is less interesting, with its rows of manorial gabled cottages, trim but uniform.

At a T-junction at the end of the village we turn right, signposted Windrush. Unexpectedly, the last cottage in the village is an old Norman chapel with a Norman doorway and tympanum.

At the fork just beyond this venerable building we go straight on
and soon reach the tree-shaded green of Windrush village. Here
again the church has some interesting Norman features, notably
the fine south doorway with a double row of beakheads and the
pillars of the chancel and nave. The church is on our right as we
leave Windrush for the Barringtons, going on for Little Barrington at the 'Fox' inn, and keeping parallel with the river Windrush.
In Little Barrington, which is prettily clustered on each side of a
stream, we turn left at the green to the church, the Norman south
doorway of which has three recessed arches beautifully moulded.
Continuing on this road past the church, we are running beside
the serpentine Windrush, though well above it, for over two
miles until we join a wider road, turning left into Burford.

On the outskirts of the town we turn left at the 'Lamb' inn
along Priory Lane to see the Elizabethan mansion built on the
site of a small priory, 'The Priory of Our Lady'. The splendid
church lies on the other side of the High Street near the river,
and is a rich composition of all periods from the Norman to the
Perpendicular Gothic. It has a number of added chapels and
among many fine tombs and monuments one of the most
magnificent is the tomb of Sir Lawrence Tanfield and his wife
(seventeenth century) in the Tanfield aisle. Near the church are
the rebuilt Grammar School, founded 1579, and the Great
Almhouses, founded 1457 and rebuilt in 1828. These and the
many ancient houses and inns, including the 'Bear and the
Crown', to be found in the High Street make an hour or two
spent in exploring Burford a rewarding experience.

We leave the town by crossing the bridge over the Windrush
on the Stow-on-the-Wold road, A424, and follow this for just over
a mile then fork right for Milton, our next objective. On reaching
Milton-under-Wychwood, to give it its full name, we bear left
at the 'Quart Pot' inn for Kingham, passing Milton's modern
church, and follow the signposts to Kingham via Bruern, looking
out for a good view of the fine mansion of Bruern Abbey on our
right just before crossing the river Evenlode and a railway.
Between here and Kingham the tower of Churchill's church is
clearly seen across fields to our right, remarkable for the fact
that it is a not unsuccessful copy of the tower of Oxford's
Magdalen College. At a T-junction at the approach to Kingham
we turn left towards the station then right into the village.

Kingham is a spacious village, its church and classical manor-house at one end, a wide green at its farther end. We go forward for Cornwell at the crossroads beyond the green and shortly fork right, again for Cornwell. Soon after passing the extensive buildings of Kingham Hill school on our right we go forward at a crossroads for Chastleton. (Less than half a mile to the right is the lovely Jacobean manor-house of Cornwell adjacent to the village, which is beautifully situated in a wooded hollow.) We cross A436 and in just over a mile reach Chastleton House, a late Elizabethan house with some superb plaster work and panelling, open to the public throughout the year daily except Wednesdays.

Our way continues beyond the house and village and straight on for Kitebrook, where we reach the main road A44. We turn left in this for only three-quarters of a mile, then leave it for a left turn to Evenlode, just short of the Four Shires Stone marking the boundaries of Oxfordshire, Gloucestershire, Worcestershire and Warwickshire. At the approach to Evenlode we bear right on the Broadwell road, which passes the church and classical manor-house, and forward in the Broadwell road at the next junction, finally turning right beyond the village and recrossing the railway and the river Evenlode to reach Broadwell. Broadwell is another pleasant village set round a wide green, through which flows a tributary of the Evenlode. We go through it on the Stow road, bearing left at the end of the green, and on reaching A429 turn left into Stow-on-the-Wold, and left again into the centre of this high-set market town, formerly of great importance. In the wide market place is the base and part of the shaft of the fourteenth-century market cross, and nearby the old church with its high Perpendicular tower.

We keep left at the market cross and then turn right at the end of the one-way street by the 'Brewery Tavern', crossing the main road towards Cheltenham. We continue on A436 for Cheltenham for a mile as far as Lower Swell, crossing the river Dickler, and just beyond the village centre turn left for the Slaughters, forking right where the road divides for Upper Slaughter. We cross the river at Upper Slaughter and turn left twice for Lower Slaughter, with a good view of the Elizabethan manor-house, a beautiful many-gabled structure in the mellow Cotswold stone. The quiet and peaceful village of Upper Slaughter gives little hint of the fierce fighting that raged here during the great civil war in the seventeenth century. Lower Slaughter is a charming village beside the stream, its houses reached by low stone and wooden bridges.

At the church we turn right and in less than half a mile reach A429, the main road in which we turn right for Bourton-on-the-Water. The shortest way to Bourton is to turn left after half a mile, then right at the post office (signposted Northleach). Bourton is altogether charming, in spite of being rather overfull at summer weekends. The river Windrush, spanned by attractive stone bridges, flows through its centre, giving Bourton its description 'Venice of the Cotswold', and there are many ancient and interesting stone houses along the wide green.

We follow the course of the Windrush past the church with its quaint late Georgian tower and dome (1785) and on reaching the main road turn right for a short distance to a disused railway bridge, beyond which we turn left, and keep left at a fork in less than a quarter of a mile for Guiting Power. In a mile and a half we leave this road for a left turn to Lower Harford, driving through a lovely stretch of the Windrush valley as we descend to Harford bridge. This time, however, we do not cross the Windrush but go straight on over the major road for Naunton, following the north bank of the Windrush into Naunton, another pretty riverside village. Here we cross the river and bear right on the other side, and on reaching A436 go forward in it for a quarter of a mile towards Cheltenham. This brings us to the 'Fox Hill' inn, where we fork right into what appears to be a private road between two stone gateposts, veering right through another gate by large stone barns, and through yet another gate by cottages. Then we descend steeply to cross a stream and turn left to climb uphill, on through Hawling Lodge, and at a T-junction right for Hawling, passing a huge stone barn and a church with neo-classical details.

At the next T-junction we turn left in the road known as the Salt Way, signposted Andoversford, and right at the next crossroads for Brockhampton, to which we continue on this grand high road with extensive views south. We go right through the straggling but picturesque village of Brockhampton and at its end go forward over the crossroads for White Hall, passing the fine mansion of Brockhampton Park. The road climbs to nearly 900 ft at the T-junction, where we turn left for Cheltenham. A row of venerable giant beeches, gnarled and twisted, lines our road as we descend gently. At another T-junction we again continue towards Cheltenham (right) and follow the signposts into the town, passing the fine Elizabethan manor-house and the church of Whittington.

The next tour is rather shorter, approximately 65 miles from Cheltenham back to Cheltenham, but there is so much of historic interest that a day is not too long to cover the distance comfortably and allow a leisurely exploration of the various places, which range from prehistoric monuments and a Roman villa to medieval towns and a notable castle. Again we take the London-Oxford road, A40, from the town centre of Cheltenham, in a mile forking right on A435 for Cirencester, soon climbing on to the rolling Wold on this road, which has the qualities of a byway. In two and a half miles we turn right briefly on A436 to Seven Springs, the source of the river Churn and for long considered to be the source of the Thames. (This is the most convenient point for motorists from Gloucester to join the tour). We return to the Cirencester road, which follows the course of the Churn all the way to the town. We, however, turn right for Elkstone after one and a half miles, crossing the Churn, here in a wooded gorge where it widens into a pond just above a waterfall. We climb steeply uphill away from the river, then turn left at the top of the hill for Colesborne on a road which runs parallel with the Churn, deep in the valley to our left, and commands grand views. We go straight on at a crossroads where Woodmancote is signposted, keeping to the high ground, and as we approach this village we bear right, then go straight on and through the centre, thence taking the next two right forks for Bagendon. From there our road runs above the glen of a tributary of the Churn and in just over a mile brings us to the pretty village of Bagendon, which lies in the valley of this stream, its little church with saddleback tower near the end of the houses just after we have forked right for Cirencester, to which we now follow the signposts.

At the outskirts of Cirencester we make for the town centre, passing on our right the gatehouse of the old Hospital of St John in Spitalgate Lane, the adjacent buildings still used as almshouses. There are two other almshouses of ancient foundation in the town, and the gateway of the old Norman abbey founded by Henry I, now forlornly the entrance to a housing estate built on the site of the abbey and its demesne. The Roman Museum near the station has a large collection of relics from the town of Corinium, developed by the Romans from the earlier settlement founded by a British tribe.

But the glory of Cirencester is the parish church of St John the Baptist, which spans the period from early Saxon times to the sixteenth century. Although only traces of Saxon work have been discovered, parts of the church rebuilt in Norman times by Henry I remain and the many beautiful features added in the following centuries blend into a superb composition. The striking Perpendicular tower built in the fifteenth century, and the great south porch, begun at the end of that century in the same style, perhaps make the greatest impression on the many visitors who come to explore and admire this splendid structure.

The early Georgian house of Cirencester Park, built by the first Earl Bathurst, is not generally on view but the present Earl Bathurst generously throws open the magnificent park to the public (pedestrians only) except on Sunday mornings. It is a few minutes' walk from the Market Place, and is entered from Cecily Hill. After exploring the town we leave Cirencester by Spitalgate Lane and cross the main road for Chedworth along the White Way. We follow this Roman road over the Wold, most junctions being signposted Chedworth, but where Withington is signposted we leave the Chedworth road and go straight on in the Roman road towards Withington over a breezy plateau and then through Withington Woods and into Withington village. We turn right into this pretty village and right again just short of the church for the Roman villa. We pass the 'Old Mill' inn and then go through the broken arch of a disused railway, after which we take the second right turning and follow the signposts to the Roman villa. This is one of the finest in England, fortunately preserved by a severe landslip, and well repays a visit. One can gain a very clear picture of life in one of these villas by an inspection of the house and its subsidiary buildings, where a fulling industry was carried on in addition to farming.

We follow the road past the villa after seeing it and go through the Chedworth Woods to Yanworth, where we go on for North-leach, thereafter following the signposts and crossing the Foss Way before entering the town, guided by the tall tower of its church. This was rebuilt in the Perpendicular style in the flourishing days of the Cotswold wool boom and has an elaborate south porch similar, but on a lesser scale, to that of Cirencester. The interior is spacious and there is a remarkable Perpendicular font with carved heads all round the bowl. We go through the market square, which is surrounded by fine wool merchants' houses, some stone and some half-timbered.

We leave the centre of Northleach by the Cheltenham road, but at the crossroads at traffic lights we turn right on A429 for Stow, then left in less than a quarter of a mile for Hampnett, where it is worth pausing at the church to see the delightful Norman chancel, which was painted in modern times, though tastefully, and on the chancel arch capitals two pelicans are carved. Thence we follow the signposts to Turkdean and Notgrove, turning up a tree-lined hill with grand views as we climb to the hilltop village of Turkdean, passing the Tudor mansion with handsome wrought-iron gates near its end, then emerge on the open plateau. We drive over the plateau, going straight on at all crossroads and past the right turnings to Notgrove village, which lies off our road, then at a T-junction we turn left for Andoversford. Half a mile beyond this junction the Notgrove Long Barrow (admission free) on the left of the road is an interesting pre-historic burial mound with a central corridor and burial chambers on each side. At the next major road we turn left towards Andoversford, but almost immediately leave it, turning right for Winchcombe. After crossing a crossroads in a quarter of a mile, our way signposted Brockhampton, we follow the signposts to Winchcombe, turning right along the old Salt Way at the next crossroads. This is a grand high road commanding extensive views across the Wold to the Malvern Hills in the far distance.

Before we reach Winchcombe we pass the entrance to Sudeley Castle, the childhood home of Princess Elizabeth after the death of her father, Henry VIII, where she lived with Queen Catherine Parr, Henry's sixth wife, who had married Lord Seymour after Henry's death. The castle is open to the public in the afternoon on Wednesdays, Thursdays and some Sundays from May to September, and usually in Easter week. Queen Catherine's apartments are shown, also her elaborate tomb in the chapel and the banqueting hall built in the middle of the fifteenth century, now in ruins but still giving some idea of its former magnificence. Although of different periods, the castle buildings are all of the mellow Cotswold stone, which gives unity to the whole.

Now we go into the lovely old market town of Winchcombe, where our way is to the left, but it is worth turning to the right to see more of the town, which contains houses of all styles and periods, chiefly in stone but some half-timbered, and a fine row of almshouses. The Perpendicular church has a lofty tower and numerous uncommonly ugly gargoyles round its roof. We pass it on the way out of the town and less than half a mile beyond it turn left for Brockhampton and Andoversford, the way also signposted Belas Knap Long Barrow. Belas Knap is one of the finest and most famous of the prehistoric memorials but can only be reached on foot. It is only a short walk, however, and well worth the effort for those interested in antiquities. We follow this lovely road for several miles, passing two interesting early manor-houses, a Tudor one at Charlton Abbots and a Jacobean one at Sevenhampton, and on reaching a T-junction turn right for Whittington and Cheltenham, either turning left to the main road in Whittington or going straight on in the lesser road.

Our next tour is a slightly longer one, about 90 miles, but it is no longer for Gloucester motorists, as the route comes back to Cheltenham via Gloucester. We visit the northern part of the Cotswold, including the famous and much frequented town of Broadway, lovely and virtually unspoilt for all that, and return by way of Bredon Hill and the ancient town of Tewkesbury, the glory of which is its abbey church. If the start is from Cheltenham we take the A435 for Evesham, turning left from the High Street at the gardens by traffic lights and bearing left on A435, and so to Pittville Circus, the centre of a later development of the town, and past the Pittville Gardens and lakes (the A435 is still well signposted). We soon come into open country with the race-course on our right backed by the Wold, and on our left look to the distant Malvern Hills. In two miles we come to Bishops Cleeve, where we turn right at the war memorial cross and just beyond the church turn left past it for Gotherington. Then at a T-junction we turn right then immediately left and continue to Gotherington, where right for Winchcombe at a junction by a war memorial. The centre of Gotherington has some attractive thatched cottages and above it to the left a clearly marked hill fort, best seen just after passing under the railway.

Now we follow this pretty road between the Wold and the Wold

The view from Birdlip Hill, near Gloucester.   (Chapter 6.)

Part of the Roman villa being excavated at Great Witcombe.   (Chapter 6.)

The central square of Stow-on-the-Wold.   (Chapter 6.)

Lower Slaughter, built alongside a tributary of the Windrush.   (Chapter 6.)

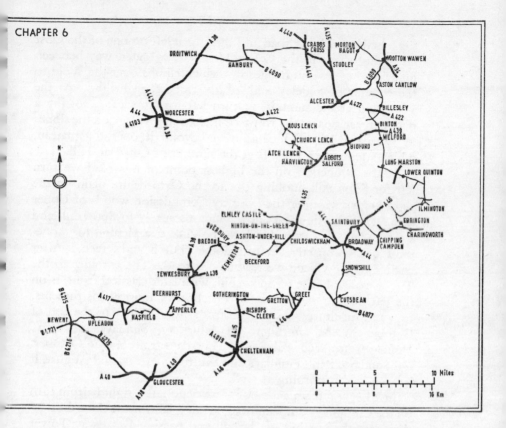

extension, passing a venerable oak on our left at the Prescott
turn. On reaching the modern spired church of Gretton we bear
right through the village and past the 'Royal Oak' inn way beyond,
soon afterwards turning left for Greet, then right at the next
т-junction and left in a few yards to bring us into Greet, set in
orchard country. In the village we turn right in Market Lane,
passing the charming and ancient manor-house, left in a quarter
of a mile in Beckett's Lane, and left again in the ensuing major
road, A46, for Broadway.

We continue on this winding road, quite unlike a main road,
for a good mile, then turn right for Hailes Abbey, an interesting
Cistercian monastery open throughout the year at a charge of
sixpence. As well as ruins of the monastic buildings and cloister,
there is a museum of sculptured fragments and tiles recovered
from the site. We return from the abbey for a hundred yards to

the junction with the road and there turn left on one of the most
intriguing roads in the Cotswold, a narrow gated way between
luxuriant hedges and hedgerows which climbs over the Wold to
the summit of Sudeley Hill, nearly 1,000 ft in height. At the
T-junction at the summit we turn left for Cutsdean, crossing a
major crossroads on the way to this charming village on the slopes
of Cutsdean Hill and continuing beyond it over the plateau,
which attains over 1,000 ft at the summit of Cutsdean Hill.

At the T-junction on the highest point of our road we turn
left for Snowshill, looking out to the Oxfordshire plain on the
right before we enter the Forestry Commission woods of Upper
Slatepits. The signposts now guide us surely to Snowshill and
we turn left on a steep hill into the village, a picturesque stone-
built one compactly set round the church and green. After
encircling the village we resume our road. The entrance to the
Tudor manor-house of Snowshill, with later classical front, is on
the left. It houses a unique collection of musical instruments,
toys and furniture, and is open from Good Friday to the end of
October in the afternoon on Saturdays, Sundays and Bank
Holidays, also Wednesdays and Thursdays from May to October.
On Sundays, Bank Holidays and Saturdays in July and August, it
is open in the morning as well.

Just beyond the manor-house we negotiate a right hairpin turn
on the Chipping Campden road, forking left for the same destina-
tion near the summit of the hill and passing Broadway Tower
after bearing left at a later junction. From the tower (which we
can climb for the sum of sixpence) there are magnificent views off
the edge of the Cotswold across the Vale of Evesham to Bredon
Hill and the Malverns, and on a clear day the faint outline of the
Welsh border hills in the far distance. Half a mile beyond the
tower we reach the main road, A44, which takes us (left) down
Broadway Hill into Broadway.

Broadway does not belie its reputation, and remains largely
unspoilt in spite of its immense popularity. Its elegant stone
houses and inns, its green fringes lined by handsome horse
chestnut trees, a beautiful sight in the flowering season, make an
impression which lingers in the memory. We drive to the end
of the town and then turn left on the Cheltenham road, A46, but
almost immediately leave it for a turning on the right for Childs-
wickham. We go straight on through the latter, keeping the

church spire far to the left and forward at the end of the village for Evesham, beckoned on by Bredon Hill.

We drive along this pretty road for two and a half miles to a main road, which we cross and fork left on the other side for Hinton-on-the-Green, soon passing the towered church and the handsome Elizabethan manor-house with a ruined gabled gate-house. Just beyond we cross the river Isbourne, and at the next fork bear right then left at the subsequent T-junction, drawing ever nearer to Bredon and looking past its northern slopes to the Malverns. Near the foot of the hill we turn left into Elmley Castle, a pretty village of timber-framed houses and a fine church, which contains an exceptionally beautiful monument to the Savage family which is well worth seeing.

We leave by the obscure turning off the main street opposite the 'Queen Elizabeth' sign, signposted Ashton-under-Hill, and follow the road round the foot of Bredon into this pretty village with some lovely thatched cottages. At the old cross and the church, dedicated to St Barbara, we go forward for Beckford, where at the church and Beckford Hall we continue for Overbury and Kemerton, still encircling Bredon Hill. At the 'Yew Tree' inn we bear left, where Bredon is signposted, into Overbury. The lane near the church leads towards Bredon's summit, with only a short walk to the top (961 ft) where the road ends, the reward splendid views encompassing the Mendips, the Welsh Mountains, the Clee Hills, the Wrekin and the Malverns in clear weather. A lane from Kemerton also leads up the hill beside the chapel.

From Kemerton we continue for Bredon and Tewkesbury, and in Bredon we fork right to see the church and river Avon. The church is an interesting one with Norman features and a striking early seventeenth-century monument to Sir Giles Reed and his wife. From Bredon we go on to Tewkesbury, passing an obelisk milestone dated 1808 and just beyond it a fourteenth-century tithe barn, now in the care of the National Trust. In Tewkesbury we find many handsome houses of all periods, notably the 'Tudor House' hotel (dated 1540) and some gabled, timbered houses with overhanging upper storeys. The old mill by the river Avon claims to date from the twelfth century and is identified with Abel Fletcher's mill in *John Halifax, Gentleman* by Mrs Craik. Finally, on no account must we leave without going into the splendid Norman abbey church of St Mary the Virgin, the second largest parish church in England, spacious and lofty, crowned by a massive central tower and richly decorated inside. It contains many interesting tombs and monuments, notably the elaborate chantry of Lord Edward Despenser surmounted by his kneeling effigy under a pinnacled canopy.

We continue past the church on the Gloucester road but after about two miles turn right on B4213 for Ledbury, going forward for Deerhurst in half a mile where the B road turns sharp left and continuing to its church, which is partly Saxon and has a rare Saxon font decorated with spiral ornament. Beyond it is an even more interesting link with Saxon times, Odda's Chapel, a Saxon building dating from 1056, now in the care of the Ministry of Works.

We return to the junction and go on through Deerhurst village on the road signposted Apperley, forking left by Apperley church, then right at a major road T-junction for Haw bridge at the crossing of the wide Severn. Half a mile on the other side of the Severn we turn left at a crossroads in sight of Tirley church and drive for about a mile along the willow-lined Ashleworth road, then turn right for Hasfield twice, passing on our right the noble mansion of Hasfield Court. Thence we bear left towards Staunton, climbing over a steep hill, forking left at a T-junction near its foot for Newent, then right at the next T-junction, right again at a major road, and left in about a third of a mile, our road signposted Upleadon and Newent. This sounds complicated but is not difficult in practice.

Now after crossing a main road and turning left at the next T-junction we soon come to the river Leadon, beside which the old Upleadon Court and the church stand. The church has an unusual half-timbered and brick tower with a shingled cap, and a fine Norman north doorway with the Lamb of God and two catlike animals on the tympanum. At the village crossroads we go forward to Newent and follow the signposts to this old market town, turning left into it on B4215. The fine timber market house is of sixteenth-century origin with a half-timbered upper storey. We follow the Gloucester road from here, passing the spired church, and continue on this B road into Gloucester and thence to Cheltenham.

Our last tour of the Wold is routed from Worcester (page 109), crossing the Vale of Evesham to explore its north-west corner and the towns and villages on the plateau and under the escarpment, including the former market centre of the Cotswold wool trade, Chipping Campden. It is a little over 80 miles in length and can easily be covered in a long afternoon, returning in the early evening. We leave Worcester by A38 as far as Droitwich, there turning right on B4090, the old Roman Salt Way, which is here signposted Alcester. After a mile and a quarter we cross the Worcester and Birmingham Canal and nearly a mile beyond this turn left for Hanbury church. We pass the red brick Queen Anne mansion of Hanbury Hall on the left, and in contrast a fine black and white farmhouse, typical of several in the parish. The church stands on the hill to the left, reached by a turning beside the stump of an old cross. It has no great architectural interest but there are some interesting monuments inside and the extensive views from the churchyard make the detour rewarding. If we do not visit the church we continue past the old cross towards Redditch.

We cross the next crossroads, signposted Astwood Bank, then follow the signposts to Redditch, crossing several crossroads, bearing left at Crabbs Cross, going over one main road and turning right immediately on a second (A448). We continue on this road to a railway (over a mile) and just beyond the bridge fork left for Studley, then right at a subsequent T-junction by the 'Barley Mow' inn, going down the main street of Studley towards Alcester. Look for the charming Queen Anne manor-house on the left in the main street, which is a mile long. At the other end we turn left just after the main road, A448, joins the high street on the right, our way signposted Morton Bagot, in half a mile crossing the Arrow. At the next junction we bear left for Morton Bagot again and continue through it to a crossroads, where we turn right for Wootton Wawen. Our next turn is right for Aston Cantlow just beyond the railway bridge, but it is worth driving on to the centre of Wootton Wawen to see 'Ye Old Bull's Head' (the date on the front is 1397), the interesting church, which has features of all periods from Saxon to seventeenth century, and nearby Wootton Hall, a fine Palladian mansion rebuilt in the late seventeenth century from an earlier Elizabethan house. It is now a residential development, with flats in the house and caravans in the park. The road going through the village, A34, is the key to Henley-in-Arden, a mile to the north, and

Stratford-on-Avon, six miles to the south. Anyone who has not seen these historic towns may care to take this opportunity to visit one or both of them.

We return to the Aston Cantlow turn, and follow the signposts to it, crossing the river Alne at an attractive willow-lined reach and following the valley as far as the village, which is very pretty with some very fine black and white timbered cottages and houses. At the T-junction beyond it we turn left for Wilmcote, the low wooded range of the Rough Hills on our immediate left, and proceed on this straight road, signposted Billesley at the next two junctions. After going through the tiny settlement of Billesley, only the hall and church of the once flourishing village surviving, we come to the main Stratford-Alcester road, which we cross for Temple Grafton. At the next crossroads we turn left for Binton and Welford, climbing up to the former on the slopes of Binton Hill, and after passing its nineteenth-century church (rebuilt on the site of a medieval one) we cross the next major road right-handed, and shortly afterwards cross the river Avon into the exceptionally lovely village of Welford. Numerous charming cottages surround its village green, in the centre of which the traditional maypole is evocative of the days of 'Merrie England'. The church, which has a Norman nave, is to the right along a turning opposite the inn and here there is another group of picturesque cottages.

At the end of the village we go straight on for Long Marston, now looking towards the Cotswold. We drive down Long Marston's single village street, just beyond the fourteenth-century church turning left for Quinton and Campden. An old building just beyond the church known as King's Lodge is one of the many in this part of the country which sheltered King Charles II during his escape after the Battle of Worcester. After leaving the village we go over a level crossing in 100 yards or so, then in less than a mile reach a major road, where we turn right towards Broadway, then left in 200 yards to resume our way to Quinton.

In Quinton we go forward for Ilmington, passing the imposing church with a lofty tower and spire, and later the turning to Hidcote Bartrim manor gardens, which are open daily, excep Tuesdays and Fridays, from the beginning of April to mid-October from 11 a.m. These beautiful gardens are well worth a visit if time allows. We continue to Ilmington on the signposted road, turning left on the Shipston road into the village and right at the next junction. The church and village green are to the right and we can encircle this part of the village and return to our road. It has some lovely stone and thatched houses, notably the gabled manor-house near the church which dates from about 1500. The church has a Norman nave but its other features are all later additions.

We go on straight uphill on the road signposted Foxcote, and reach the top of Windmill Hill with grand views to the left across the Stour valley. We continue to Charingworth, turning right at the foot of the steep descent, and thence follow the road through Ebrington into Chipping Campden. We enter the town beside the magnificent Perpendicular 'wool' church, its high tower crowned by battlements and pinnacles. Just beyond are the ruins of the once sumptuous mansion built in the early part of the seventeenth century by a former Lord Mayor of London, a wealthy cloth merchant. His descendant, who defended it for the Royalists in the Civil War, had it destroyed to prevent it from falling into Parliamentarian hands.

We turn left into the town to see its fine market hall, its merchants' houses, grammar school founded in Tudor times, town hall and almshouses. Although the houses are of all periods from late fourteenth century to early eighteenth century, the mellow stone houses are in perfect harmony and bear eloquent testimony to the importance of the town when it was the centre of the Cotswold wool trade. We go straight through the main street on the Weston-sub-Edge road, bearing right at the end of the town, again for Weston, then in half a mile turn left at the crossroads for Willersey, and right fork for the latter in half a mile. At the next crossroads, however, we turn right for Saintbury and go through this village to the next major road, A46, where right for half a mile and where the main road bends sharp right we go straight on for Honeybourne, crossing B4035 after a quarter of a mile. We follow this Roman road, Ryknild Street, which takes us, straight as an arrow, to Bidford, crossing the Avon into it over the fine fifteenth-century stone bridge. The handsome town and church are to the right, but our way is left on the Evesham road, A439, so we must make a detour if we have not previously seen the town.

We follow the Evesham road for about three miles to Harvington, passing on the way the Jacobean gabled Salford Hall behind a timbered and stone barn in Abbot's Salford. In Harvington we turn right just short of the church for the Lenches, in half a mile crossing A435. We go straight on at the Sheriff's Lench turn, and through the picturesque Atch Lench, a village of black and white cottages, and on to Church Lench, where right to Rous Lench. These are all villages among the extensive orchards of the Lench Hills. At Rous Lench we pass a red brick tower and then the black and white Tudor manor-house, both on the right of the road. The church was originally built in Norman times and retains an elaborate Norman doorway, three massive pillars and arches in the nave, and its Norman chancel arch. Now we continue towards Inkberrow, but where the Worcester signposts supervene we follow these back to Worcester.

CHAPTER SEVEN

THE WYE AND THE WESTERN HILLS

THE BORDER COUNTY of Herefordshire is remarkably unspoilt. Famed far and wide for its Hereford cattle and its cider apple orchards, its traditions are agricultural and no mining districts or great industrial complexes mar its beautiful scenery. The broad river Wye flows across the county in a generally south-easterly direction, passing through the county town and receiving the waters of many lesser rivers and streams on its progress to the junction with the Severn below Chepstow.

The wide river valleys are bounded by a series of green wooded hills, though towards the boundary with Wales the hills become more bold and rugged. The abundant woodlands have through the ages provided the building material for the beautiful 'black and white' towns and villages typical of the Marcher country, and we visit many of these delightful places in the course of the following tours.

Hereford, the county town and cathedral city, is situated near the centre of the county and therefore makes an admirable base for touring, offering plenty of accommodation of all kinds. In addition it has enough of interest in its own right to demand exploration. Its pride, the cathedral, is not only a splendid example of medieval architecture but has two unique treasures. These are the ancient Mappa Mundi, a map of the world as then known, believed to have been drawn in the early fourteenth century, and the Chained Library in Jacobean wooden presses, which is the largest in the country and contains a priceless collection of illuminated manuscripts and rare books.

The first cathedral in stone was built soon after the murder of King Ethelbert in 792 by Offa, King of the Mercians, and dedicated to the martyred saint, as he later became (page 102). The earliest parts of the present cathedral, the choir and the south transept, date from the last quarter of the eleventh century,

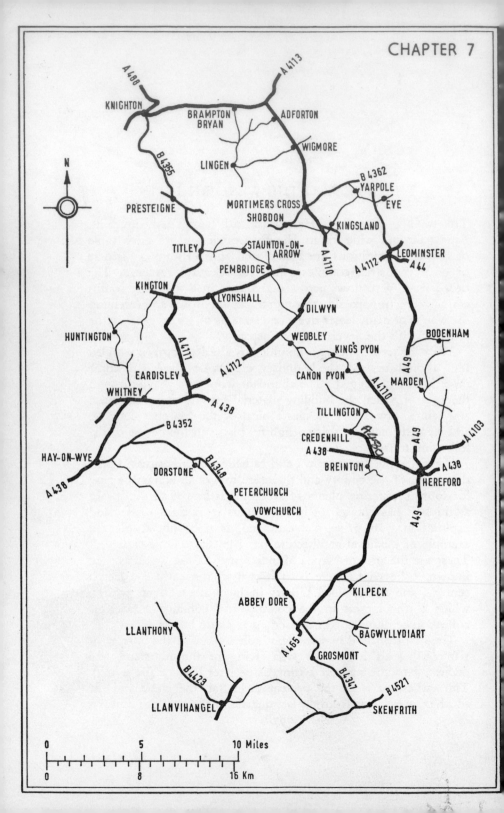

while the massive Norman columns and arches of the nave are legacies from the following century. Later additions harmonize perfectly with the Norman nucleus and there are many medieval monuments, most of them to be found in the choir.

All Saints church, in the High Street, also possesses a Chained Library, though this is a relatively small one. Near the church, in the centre of the High Town, the beautiful black and white half-timbered 'Old House' is a famous landmark. Built in 1621, it contains an outstanding collection of Jacobean furniture and fascinating objects of the period, so that the visitor can visualize the daily routine of contemporary life.

Founded a few years earlier, in 1614, as a home for old soldiers and family servants, Coningoby Hospital survives in nearby Widemarsh Street, and behind it is a fragment of the Black Friars monastery. There are several other hospitals established in the seventeenth century and one originally of medieval foundation (1290), Giles Hospital in St Owen Street, not far from the attractive Castle Pool and Green. Two personalities of the theatre were born in Hereford—David Garrick and Nell Gwynne. By a strange quirk of fate, the grandson of Nell and King Charles II became Bishop of Hereford!

Our first tour, approximately 70 miles in length, leaves Hereford by A438, signposted Hay, and we continue for Hay at the junction with A4110, then a quarter of a mile beyond the junction with A480 turn left for Breinton, turning right at the next junction for Breinton Common. We see the red cliffs above the Wye across the fields, the dense hanging woods marking its course, and after going through luxuriant orchards come nearer to the river bank. On rejoining the main road we continue for a mile along it, then turn right for Kenchester, but after rather less than half a mile we turn right again on the road signposted Credenhill. Credenhill lies on A480, which we cross right-handed (the left turn is visible immediately, signposted Tillington) and follow the foot of Creden Hill (720 ft), crowned by a prehistoric hill fort.

At the crossroads by the 'Bell' inn in Tillington we turn left for Weobley, driving through the fine wooded hills, the well-shaped wooded peak of Round Oak Hill (790 ft) on our right. This lovely ride takes us in about six miles to Weobley, one of the most beautiful 'black and white' villages in the country, its

imposing high-spired church contrasting strangely with the
rows of cottages. At a T-junction in the village we turn right for
Leominster and on reaching A4112 turn left towards Hay and
right in a quarter of a mile for Pembridge, keeping left at a fork
by a farm pond. Here we are in orchard country and we go
through some fine apple orchards, as well as belts of handsome
mature trees, especially in the park of Broxwood Court, where
there are some gigantic exotic trees.

At the next major road we turn right for Lyonshall and in this
village turn left for Eardisley along a ridge road giving views to
the Black Mountains of Wales, turning left again at a major road,
which takes us into Eardisley. We drive down the main street
between rows of pleasant black and white cottages to the church,
where the splendid Norman font in the Celtic tradition has
carved figures wearing the pleated tunics and 'trews' characteristic
of this period. From the church we return to the village crossroads and turn left for Woodseaves, continuing to Whitney by
the bank of the Wye, where right on the main road beside the
river. We drive alongside the bank for about one and a half
miles as far as the 'Rhydspence' inn and the Welsh boundary
(round the corner) and turn hard right up a steep and narrow lane
just short of the inn, a pretty road through the hanging woods
above the Wye. Care is needed on the descent. We go forward
at a fork by a farm, bear right at the next junction uphill, and right
again at the top along the ridge, again looking down on the Wye.
At a crossroads in about a mile we turn left for Newchurch,
right at the next two junctions for Huntington, and from
Huntington follow the signposts to Kington.

We reach Kington at its fine spired church, where we turn right
into the town, which is situated on the river Arrow and has
some good timbered houses. We go through the town on the
Hereford road but where this turns right we go forward for
Titley on the Presteigne road, driving beside Eywood Park,
recognized by its several ornamental lakes, just before reaching
Titley. Here we turn right at the end of the village, beyond the
church, on the road to Staunton-on-Arrow, which passes below
the well-wooded slopes of Wapley Hill, rising to over 1,000 ft on
our left. After two miles we turn right amidst apple orchards into
Staunton and at the first crossroads beyond the church, which
is only just over a century old, we go forward for Pembridge.

At the next junction we turn right past a disused railway station, soon crossing the broad river Arrow into Pembridge, driving through a street of fine timbered houses towards the church, turning right at a T-junction and left at the picturesque black and white 'New Inn', which faces the ancient timber market hall on eight pillars. The church has a quaint detached belfry tower in stages like a pagoda.

We go on past the market hall and forward at a crossroads in the way signposted Dilwyn. In a mile, just short of the next junction, look left for the superb timbered manor-house of Luntley Court, built in the late seventeenth century, and on the opposite side of the road the picturesque gabled black and white pigeon house which is contemporary with the manor-house. We continue to Dilwyn and drive into the village centre near the church, the short sturdy tower of which is crowned by a rather unharmonious spire, turning right at the little green with a single pink chestnut, and shortly bearing left, both roads signposted Hereford. At the subsequent junction in a quarter of a mile, however, we turn right for King's Pyon, continuing to this village, turning left at an unsignposted T-junction, and following round the edge of a hill (we are surrounded on all sides by wooded hills).

In King's Pyon we go on towards Canon Pyon, passing another pigeon house near the church, and turning left at the subsequent crossroads. Canon Pyon lies under Pyon Hill, a pretty wooded conical hill which looks across the valley to a similar peak called Robin Hood's Butts. From there we soon come to the main road, and it only remains to turn right in it and drive back into Hereford, with a good view of the cathedral as we breast the final slope before entering the outskirts of the city.

The next tour is rather longer than the previous one, about 90 miles in all. It traverses the county westwards to the Welsh boundary, just crossing it to Knighton, a typical Welsh border town, visiting several historic homes on the outward journey and returning to Hereford by way of the ancient town of Leominster. From Hereford's centre we take the Leominster road, A49, for nearly four miles, which brings us well into the open country, then turn right for Marden, going through Moreton and crossing a level crossing and the river Lugg before reaching Marden, into which we turn left. We pass on the left the turning to the church which is on the bank of the Lugg and is famous for being the burial place of King Ethelbert after his murder in 792 while on a visit to King Offa of Mercia, whose palace is believed to have been in the vicinity. King Ethelbert's body was later removed to Hereford, where he was canonized and shares the dedication of the present cathedral with the Virgin Mary.

At the end of the village we fork left for Leominster and continue to the 'Volunteer' inn, where we go forward for Litmarsh, and at the next two junctions continue for Bodenham, now mostly in orchard country, which is later interspersed with hop gardens. The road eventually brings us to a T-junction, where we turn left towards Leominster, joining A417 at 'England's Gate' inn in about a mile, but we leave this main road in less than half a mile for a turning on the right for Risbury. At the first fork, in about a mile and a half, we fork left for Humber, and left again at a subsequent junction. Later we fork right for Bromyard on a road which follows the line of the old Roman road which skirts Leominster to the east. We go straight along this road, crossing all crossroads, including one main road, with good views ahead to the Shropshire hills. When we leave the vicinity of Leominster the road is signposted Ludlow, and on reaching A49 we turn right along it towards Ludlow.

Soon the road runs beside the fine timbered park and orna-mental lake of Berrington Hall, a late Georgian mansion built by Henry Holland, with especially fine ceilings, and now in the care of the National Trust. The park was landscaped by 'Capability Brown'. The house and gardens are both open to the public from Easter to the end of September on Wednesday afternoons (and Bank Holiday Mondays). At the end of Berring-ton park we turn left for Eye Manor. This is another interesting house, built a century earlier than Berrington Hall, with fine plasterwork and period furniture. It is open in the afternoon from Easter Sunday to the end of September on Sundays, Wednesdays, Thursdays and Saturdays, as well as Bank Holiday Mondays and Tuesdays, and on Saturdays and Sundays during October, and visitors are welcome to picnic on the lawns. The adjacent church has two imposing marble monuments of Knights of the Cornewalles family of Berrington Hall, also an exceptional Jacobean carved wooden pulpit.

We return right at a T-junction at the next hamlet after leaving

Eye, then left in about 200 yards beside a black and white cottage for Yarpole, turning right into Yarpole at another T-junction. At Yarpole post office we bear left, passing the church, which has a detached belfry tower similar to that of Pembridge, with a stone lower stage crowned by a timber belfry with a shingled cap. We cross the ensuing major road to see yet another National Trust property, Croft Castle, open to the public in the afternoon from Easter Monday to the end of September on Wednesdays, Thursdays, Saturdays, Sundays and Bank Holiday Mondays, also at weekends during October. The manor is said to have been in the possession of the Croft family since the time of Edward the Confessor, and the castle, which is mentioned in the Domesday Book, is still lived in by members of that family.

We return from the castle to the major road, in which we turn right for Mortimer's Cross. If there is not time to visit the castle on this occasion there is a clear view of its exterior from this road to the right beyond the exit gate. In another mile we pass on the left the handsome Wren-style Lucton School, which has a statue of its founder in full-bottomed wig in a niche over the entrance. We cross the river Lugg at Mortimer's Cross, which derives its name from a fierce battle in the Wars of the Roses, fought in 1461, the Yorkists being led by Edward, Earl of March, later Edward IV. We go over the crossroads but in about 250 yards turn right into Mortimer's Forest along a very pretty valley road through the forest, recrossing the river Lugg shortly before reaching a T-junction, where we turn left for Lingen, the densely afforested Shobdon Hill Wood rising to over 1,000 ft to our left as we continue to Lingen. The lanes here are beautiful but narrow, so caution is needed.

We turn right at an unsignposted T-junction into a wider road which takes us into Lingen in just over half a mile. At the central junction just short of Lingen church we turn right for Wigmore on a road which rises to 735 ft and gives splendid views to the surrounding hills. We descend through woods and eventually reach a major road, in which we turn left into Wigmore and drive through the village, beyond it passing on our left the castle mound and a fragment of surviving masonry. We follow this pretty lesser main road to Adforton, there going on for Brampton Bryan, the open views now northward to the Shropshire hills, turning left on reaching A4113. Brampton Bryan lies under

Coxall Knoll, a well-shaped wooded hill nearly 800 ft high. It is crowned by a prehistoric hill fort which is claimed to be the last site held by Caratacus before his defeat by the Romans. This camp, however, is not visible from the village, where we bear right at the attractive green for Knighton. We turn right again at the first signposted junction for Bucknell, crossing the river Teme, and left for Weston just before a level crossing. Our road now follows the north bank of the Teme, which winds through the lovely valley just below us all the way to Knighton (over four miles).

We cross the railway and river to enter the town, turning left on the Presteigne road (the town centre with tall clock tower is to the right). The road to Presteigne is a fine hill road rising to over 1,000 ft with the long line of Radnor Forest to our right. We turn left into the town and go straight on towards Leominster. The church lies down the picturesque Broad Street, which ends at a pretty corner by the river Lugg. Our road is later signposted Mortimer's Cross but we leave this road at Shobdon, two miles short of Mortimer's Cross.

Shobdon is an attractive village with the interesting fragments of its old Norman church and a fascinating mid-eighteenth-century successor, both reached by the drive of Shobdon Court, which starts opposite the village inn. The Norman fragments, known as 'The Arches' were re-erected a quarter of a mile beyond the present church in the park, which has several lakes and many fine trees. The arches and columns are richly carved with animals and figures in the Celtic tradition, similar to those at Eardisley and Kilpeck. But the later church is a real curiosity, which has been described as a unique essay in Georgian Rococo Gothic, retaining only the tower of the medieval church. Inside, the ornamental pointed arches, the pointed pew ends with inserted quatrefoils and other 'Gothic' features are all painted blue and white, as is the whole church interior. Only the medieval font, with its spirited carved lions round the stem, strikes a note of contrast.

We leave the village at its far end by the war memorial cross on the road signposted Kingsland and follow the signposts for Kingsland, at a main road turning left towards Knighton, almost immediately right in a minor road beside an orchard, and right at a subsequent T-junction. We drive through the long

Chipping Campden's main street, seen through an arch of the market house. (Chapter 6.)

The maypole on the green, Welford-on-Avon. (Chapter 6.)

Upleadon church, showing the unusual brick and timber tower and the Norman doorway. (Chapter 6.)

Arlington Row, Bibury, beside the river Coln. (Chapter 6.)

village street of Kingsland, noting the unusually massive tower buttresses with sculptured panels as we pass the church, and at the next signposted crossroads turn left for Leominster and this time go into the formerly important town, once reputed to have the best wool market in England. It retains some good timbered houses of ancient date and also many handsome Georgian houses and old inns. The medieval Drapers Lane looks as it must have done when it was built. The former market hall was rebuilt on a site beside the recreation ground near the church in the nineteenth century and retains the original oak columns. It is now known as Grange House.

The priory church of St Peter and St Paul, near the bank of the river Lugg, retains the splendid Norman nave and west doorway of the original priory church, beside it the thirteenth-century townspeople's nave, and to the south of that the beautiful Decorated south aisle with richly ornamented windows. The top stages of the tower were added in the fifteenth century in the Perpendicular style. Even though we are near the end of our tour, it is well worth sparing time to see this outstanding architectural gem.

Now we leave for Hereford, but soon after crossing the river Arrow turn right on an unsignposted road between two isolated houses, climbing on to the lower slopes of Dinmore, at the next junction continuing for Hereford, finally reaching the major road after a lovely ride under Dinmore Hill. There we turn left and so back to Hereford.

The third tour from Hereford, approximately 80 miles long if the return is made via Abbey Dore, explores the outliers of the Black Mountains and the beautiful valley in which Llanthony Priory is set, and returns through the quieter but equally lovely Golden Valley, visiting several historic places situated along the route. We leave Hereford by A49 for Ross-on-Wye but after crossing the Wye fork right on the Abergavenny road, A465, and leave this road in turn after a mile and a half, forking left for Haywood and Callow. After another two miles we fork right for Tram Inn and on reaching a wider road go forward in it for Ross, forking right for Kilpeck at the next fork in half a mile. Now we continue to Kilpeck, turning right at the next T-junction and going over a crossroads to see the famous Norman church, with a richly sculptured south doorway in the Celtic tradition with the characteristic animals and warriors in tunics and trews. The west window is richly ornamented on the outside and there are grotesque corbel heads all round the walls. Inside there are two Norman chancel arches and a vaulted apse, a large Norman font and a curious holy water stoup clasped by two arms and hands. The castle mound next to the church is all that remains of the Norman fortress.

We return from the church to the first junction, where we turn right for Bagwyllydiart and continue to this small hamlet, following the signposts for Orcop at the next two junctions. At the junction at the 'New Inn' we go forward, then right just beyond the inn and left at a subsequent fork by a chapel for St Weonards along a high shelf with long views to the hills south of Hereford to our left. Near the foot of the hill we turn right at an unsignposted fork, and right again at the next T-junction in about three-quarters of a mile, at the next T-junction at a common turning left into a wider road. These are all pretty roads among the tumbled hills which give such variety to the landscapes in this part of the county.

When we reach a major road at the 'Broad Oak' inn we turn right for Skenfrith, less than two miles away, driving alongside the bank of the Monnow in the last half mile before crossing it into Skenfrith. We turn right by the considerable ruin of the castle, which has a circular keep surrounded by a square outer wall with round angle towers, and is open daily to visitors at a fee of sixpence, and go on to the church, a late Norman one with the typical Monmouthshire low tower and timber belfry with shingled cap.

At the next junction in the village we turn right for Grosmont, continuing along the lovely Monnow valley and later under hanging woods. The interesting castle of Grosmont, now in the care of the Ministry of Works, is also open daily at a fee of sixpence. It was built at the end of the twelfth century and large fragments of the original stonework remain, as well as a decorative chimney of the later fourteenth-century buildings. The entrance to the castle is opposite the church, which is also worth a visit. It is a large cruciform one, mainly in the Early English style of Gothic, though it was begun in Norman times and has an octagonal tower and tall spire.

We go on through the village past the old stone market house, then near the end of the houses fork left, and left again at a subsequent T-junction, both roads signposted Abergavenny. The 1,955 ft peak of the Sugar Loaf is imminent ahead and the whole range of the Black Mountains bounds our horizon. Our road is later signposted Llanvihangel Crucorney and on reaching a major road at Llanvihangel we turn left, then right in a quarter of a mile for Llanthony on B4423. The entrance to Llanvihangel Court, a Tudor manor-house occasionally open to visitors on summer Sundays and Bank Holidays in the afternoon, is opposite the church just beyond this turning.

We now follow this wonderful B road right up the valley all the way to Llanthony Priory, running alongside the river Honddu, and hemmed in by steep hills on both sides. A considerable fragment of the priory church survives, including the towers and part of the nave. Some of the monastic buildings are incorporated in the adjacent farm and hotel, while the little parish church is a Norman one contemporary with the priory. We continue up the valley beyond the priory for Capel-y-ffin, a narrow but good road with passing places, only built up in recent years, which goes up to the head of the valley and over the watershed, descending to Hay-on-Wye. As it traverses the bare moorlands beside the source of the Honddu it reaches a height of nearly 1,800 ft and as we breast the summit a magnificent panorama is spread before us as we look across the Wye valley to the seemingly endless ranges of the Welsh mountains. Then we descend gradually beside Hay Forest, mainly planted with coniferous trees, turning right into Hay on A438, but leaving it on the outskirts for B4348, signposted Vowchurch. We pass the later mansion on the site of the castle (there is little else of note to see in Hay), thereafter bearing right and going on for the Golden Valley, taking the right fork for Peterchurch (still on B4348).

We now drive along the Golden Valley on a very pretty road between wooded hills, aiming for Peterchurch. We pass Dorstone's square-towered church (Dorstone's only other notable feature is one and a half miles off the road at the top of Dorstone Hill—a massive prehistoric burial chamber known as Arthur's Stone) and continue to Peterchurch on the other side of the river Dore. The parish church of St Peter is another interesting Norman one, its most interesting feature the three Norman arches of the chancel. A rare survival is the original stone altar in the apse, while the solid Norman font has characteristic moulding.

From Peterchurch we can return to Hereford via Vowchurch and Abbey Dore on B4347, or more directly by a cross-country route, turning left over the hills less than half a mile beyond Peterchurch church for Stockley Hill. We climb up the steep hill, then over the top, where the views are across the Wye valley to the Malvern Hills and Hereford is visible in the distance. From here we have no difficulty in finding our way back to the city.

If, however, Abbey Dore has not previously been visited, it is worth taking the longer route to see this fine abbey church, which has become the parish church. Although the existing church consists only of tower, transepts and choir, these are spacious and a beautiful example of the Early English style of Gothic architecture, with high pointed arches and lancet windows, We retrace our way for a short distance after seeing the church and then turn right to cross the river Dore and go forward for Hereford.

CHAPTER EIGHT

TO THE MALVERN AND SHROPSHIRE HILLS

WORCESTERSHIRE acts as a bridge between the Midlands and the West Country, the Severn running from north to south of the county and acting as a natural division between the larger eastern portion, which looks to the Birmingham complex, and the smaller area to the west of the river, where the traditions of the West Country are firmly maintained. It is a county of grand wooded hills and of extensive orchards, the latter concentrated mainly in the Vale of Evesham.

Since in this book we are exploring the West Country, our tours will be in the country to the west of the Severn, for which the county town of Worcester is an excellent centre, with ample accommodation. Worcester is also the starting point for the tour to the Vale of Evesham and the north-west corner of the Cotswold which falls into Chapter 6.

The cathedral of this historic town, seen to best advantage across the river, was founded in 680 and this early church was rebuilt and enlarged by St Oswald towards the end of the tenth century. The present structure was begun by St Wulstan in 1084 and of his church the crypt is the most impressive survival, for most of the remaining Norman features, including the lofty chapter house, were not completed until after his death. The choir and nave were later substantially rebuilt in the Gothic style.

Of the many ancient monuments, the tomb of King John in the centre of the choir attracts most attention. It is a richly carved table tomb, carrying what is considered to be a life-like marble effigy of that unpopular monarch, who died little more than a year after the signing of Magna Carta. The beautiful chantry chapel in the late Gothic style was erected in 1504 over the tomb of Prince Arthur, the elder brother of King Henry VIII.

Close by the cathedral on College Green, entered on the

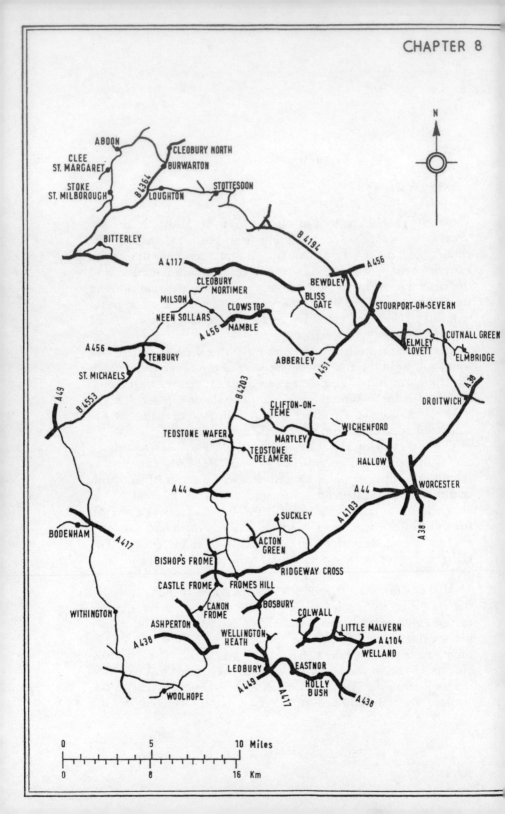

east side through the archway under the medieval Edgar Tower, are the ruins of the monastery guest house and the splendid refectory, restored as the hall of the King's School. Ironically, the school was endowed by King Henry VIII in 1541 out of the funds appropriated from the monastery at its dissolution. The old bishop's palace, formerly the deanery, also survives as the Worcester Diocesan Church House.

There are several other medieval churches in the city and a number of hospitals, or almshouses, among which is the Commandery, founded by Wulstan in 1085. The fine timbered hall has a minstrels gallery and is open to visitors all the year from Mondays to Fridays. The Greyfriars in Friars Street, a timbered house built in 1480 for the Franciscan Friary, is also open to the public from June to October on the first Thursday afternoon in each month.

The Guildhall in High Street is of another age. It was completed in 1723 from a design by Thomas White, a local pupil of Sir Christopher Wren, and follows unmistakably the tradition of the master. On the facade are statues of Charles I and Charles II, and of Queen Anne, and in the centre of the doorway arch, perhaps in token of Worcester's loyalty to the Royalist cause, the head of Cromwell, nailed by the ears, is carved in stone.

There are many beautiful black and white houses of ancient origin to be found in the city centre, of which two of the most notable are Queen Elizabeth's House, with an open gallery on the upper floor from which the Queen is reputed to have addressed the citizens, and King Charles's House, one of the many in which Charles II took refuge after his defeat at Worcester. Last, but not least, the Royal Worcester porcelain factory, where the beautiful and world famous china has been manufactured since the mid-eighteenth century, is well worth a visit. Early examples of the porcelain are displayed in a museum attached to the factory. A day is certainly not too long for a thorough exploration of Worcester's fascinating links with its past history.

Now for our first tour, which covers a distance of just under 85 miles, its highlights the volcanic Malvern Hills and the picturesque town of Ledbury. We leave Worcester by A443 for Stourport and Bewdley and follow this road for just over three miles, and in Hallow take the second turning on the left by a large garage, half a mile beyond the spired church. At the next two junctions we keep left for Wichenford, turning left again into the village, soon passing the church on our right, which though rebuilt has some medieval work and several handsome monuments and tombs inside. A mile beyond the village we come to a major road, in which we turn right for Martley. Its medieval towered church, which also contains some good monuments, is just off the road to the left before we reach a T-junction in the village. Here we turn right, then left, for Clifton-on-Teme, to which this B road takes us, going through rolling green country and crossing the river Teme at Ham Bridge.

Clifton itself is situated on high ground well above the river and almost two miles beyond the crossing. It is a picturesque village with a medieval church, just beyond which we turn left for Whitbourne and continue on this hilly road, finally descending beside a deep gorge to a junction, where we turn right for Sapey Bridge. Now we are making for the orchard country of the Tedstones and so we bear right at the next two junctions signposted Tedstone and thereafter the road takes us straight on to Tedstone Delamere. We pass on our right the mansion of Tedstone Court, set in a lovely park with many graceful exotics, and below it on the hill is the small church. Here the road bends left and in less than a mile brings us to the T-junction at Tedstone Wafer post office, where we turn right, then in less than a quarter of a mile left, and left again at the next junction on the edge of a hill in about a mile. We continue on this road, passing on our right the isolated church, a modern spired one, of Edvin Loach. The ruins of the medieval church are in the churchyard. Shortly after this we see on our left the modern Saltmarshe Castle, a large castle-like mansion.

On reaching a major road about two miles from the last junction we turn right and follow this high road to the outskirts of Bromyard. At the first signposted junction we fork left for Worcester and Malvern but in a quarter of a mile turn right on the other side of the river bridge. This intimate little road takes us on for miles over rolling and fertile farming country. We go forward over all crossroads, following the Bishop's Frome signposts at two points but then going forward for Frome's Hill, leaving the Bishop's Frome road. We cross the main road at Frome's Hill left-handed by the 'Wheatsheaf' hotel, our way signposted Bosbury.

Ledbury's timbered market house on chestnut wood pillars. (Chapter 8.)

The ruins of the priory church at Llanthony. (Chapter 7.)

Salwarpe manor-house, near Droitwich, the oldest part of which dates from the sixteenth century. (Chapter 8.)

The massive walls and angle towers of Skenfrith Castle. (Chapter 7.)

We now have magnificent views east to the Malvern Hills and to our right as far as the Welsh mountains. Aiming for Bosbury, we turn left at a T-junction, go straight on at a subsequent junction, then bear right at a later one. Now we continue to Bosbury, which lies on another main road, which we cross left-handed for Wellington Heath. The fine medieval church and most of the village, where there are some quaint old houses, are to the right along the main road. We bear right at the next T-junction, left at the following one, and in Wellington Heath right at the triangle and oak tree for Ledbury and thereafter continue into Ledbury.

Ledbury is a handsome little town, once with an important cloth making industry. There are many ancient timbered houses in its long main street and the streets leading from it, but its pride is the beautiful half-timbered market house on sixteen chestnut wood pillars which stands in the wide market place. Nearby is the chapel of the medieval almshouses, farther along the main street the picturesque 'Feathers' hotel, and leading from the market place the charming timbered houses in the narrow Church Lane, taking the eye to the imposing church dating from Norman times, its detached tower crowned by a tall graceful spire.

We leave Ledbury by the Worcester road, but shortly fork right on A438 for Eastnor, where we shall find the entrance to Eastnor Castle at the T-junction in the village, whence our way is right for Bromsberrow. The Castle was built in the Regency period in the style of a medieval baronial castle, and has a wonderful collection of pictures, tapestries and armour. It is open on Sunday afternoons from June to September and also on Bank Holiday Mondays.

We now continue towards Bromsberrow, bearing left at a junction, then left again at a T-junction where Tewkesbury is signposted, but right almost immediately past Bromsberrow Place. At the next junction we bear left, then go straight on for Holly Bush where Great Malvern is signposted to the right (our road is marked 'unsuitable for heavy traffic'). When we come to a main road we cross it and drive along a fine shelf on the slopes of the Malverns, but in just over half a mile we must look carefully for a steep narrow road on the right (if we miss it we shall come to a large quarry and must retrace our way). This little road, after plunging headlong downhill, brings us out on to a wide common and we drive over this, with the bold ridge of the

Malverns imminent on our left, as far as Welland crossroads by
the spired church. There we turn left to Little Malvern, passing
the priory church and climbing to the top of the hill, where we
turn left at a hairpin bend towards the Herefordshire Beacon
crowned by an extensive prehistoric camp with well preserved
entrenchments. We continue past the hotel at the top of the hill
on the Ledbury road, now having crossed the ridge, then turn
right in just over a mile on A4105 for Colwall. Now we follow
the line of the hills on their west side. We continue to Colwall
and there, after crossing the railway, turn left for Coddington,
later passing the old parish church of Colwall, situated three-
quarters of a mile from the main part of the village near the
railway. At the next junction after the church we turn right for
Coddington, but thenceforward follow the signposts for Mathon
and Cradley. Where Mathon is signposted to the right, however,
we keep straight on for Ridgeway Cross.

Ridgeway Cross lies on a pleasant little main road, A4103, which
takes us directly back to Worcester through fertile farming and
orchard country and one or two quiet villages.

The second tour, a longer one of 100 miles, goes further
afield to the upper reaches of the Severn and the southern hills
of Shropshire. We leave Worcester by A38 and follow it as far as
Droitwich. A mile short of Droitwich it is worth turning off to
the left by the prominent 'Copcut Elm' inn to see one of the
finest half-timbered houses in the country, Salwarpe Court.
Although it is not open to the public there is an unobstructed view
from the road of the exterior, which is little changed since it was
built, the earliest gabled part dating from the mid-sixteenth
century. The road ends at the church, so we must return to A38
and continue to Droitwich. We must spare time to turn into the
pleasant centre of Droitwich if this is our first visit. Its traditional
salt trade was important at the time of the Domesday Book,
and possibly dates back as far as Roman times, while the brine
baths contributed to its later development as a spa and health
resort. There are some fine old black and white houses in the
older part of the town and two of the four medieval parish
churches have survived. Resuming our route, we cross the river
and go under the railway bridge on A38, but on the other side of
the railway bridge we turn left immediately into Crutch Lane, a
minor road going steeply uphill.

At the first signposted fork we bear left for Elmbridge, and left again at the next junction, this time for Cutnall Green, passing Elmbridge church and noting the fine Norman south doorway as we pass. We turn left once again for Cutnall Green, then in less than half a mile right and soon come to Cutnall Green. Our way from Droitwich has so far been along peaceful lanes lined with handsome mature trees. At Cutnall Green we are briefly in a more urban development on a major road as we turn right at 'Ye Old Chequers Inne'. However, we leave this road in a few yards for the left turn for Elmley Lovett and resume our way in the quiet lanes. We continue to Elmley Lovett, bearing left to pass close to its spired church, where Sneads Green is signposted, then right at the next junction for Hartle-bury. We go straight on over three crossroads, the second a main road, and on reaching a main road T-junction we turn right and soon reach the outskirts of Stourport-on-Severn. This is a largely modern town which grew up at the terminus of the Staffordshire and Worcestershire Canal after its completion in the second half of the eighteenth century. Its warehouses, factories and quays which line the left bank of the Severn near its confluence with the Stour are evidence of its industrial prosperity.

In the town we turn left on A451 and after crossing the Stour left again for the town centre, thence following the signposts for town centre and Great Witley, a left turn for Great Witley taking us to the crossing of the Severn. Just over a quarter of a mile beyond the river we keep right on A451 at a main fork, then in just over another mile we turn sharp right at a telephone box for Heightington. This road takes us over orchard country through the hamlet of Heightington to Bliss Gate, where we go over the crossroads at the 'Bliss Gate' inn for Far Forest. At the next T-junction we turn left for Clows Top, cross a later main road, A456, and in less than a quarter of a mile turn left for Buckeridge.

Here we have a grand view to the Clee Hills as we descend sharply, then on the straight road dive into a little combe, finally winding down to a river valley and as we reach dense woodlands turn left at a T-junction. We soon leave the woods and come to a major road, B4202, where we turn right for Cleobury Mortimer, thereafter following the signposts to Cleobury, guided by the distant spire of its church in the valley ahead. Our road takes us across the river Rea and through the main street of the pleasant

little town of Cleobury Mortimer, attractively lined on one side
of the road by a row of lime trees. The medieval church retains
its Norman tower, crowned by a later spire. A short distance
beyond it we turn left at a crossroads, our way rather surprisingly
signposted Tenbury.

We continue on this pretty road through orchard country,
mainly in sight of the Clee Hills, following the signposts to
Milson, its spired church a landmark, thence continuing to
Tenbury, which is well signposted. We turn left by the 'Rose and
Crown' inn to cross the river Teme into Tenbury Wells, right at
the 'Swan' hotel, and drive down the main street, where there are
some good black and white timbered houses. The 'Wells' of
its name derives from the medicinal spring discovered in the
mid-nineteenth century, when a pump room and baths were
erected. The church was rebuilt in the eighteenth century to
replace the medieval one which was almost entirely destroyed by a
disastrous flood in that century. At the end of the town we keep
right again for Leominster, soon running over a wide common to
St Michaels.

We proceed towards Leominster for several miles on this
major road, B4553, looking across to the mountains of Wales,
and at a junction with A49 we veer sharp left away from the main
road. If we have not previously seen Leominster (page 105),
at this point it is only a mile distant. Our pleasant minor road
takes us straight on in the direction of Hereford, crossing all
crossroads, including two major ones, finally bearing right at a
triangular junction for Bodenham. Thence we go on for Hereford
via Bodenham, turning left in the main road, A417, for a short
half mile then leave it at 'England's Gate' inn to pursue our way
towards Hereford. Unless we specially wish to visit Hereford
on this occasion, however, after two miles we fork left by the
'New Inn' for Withington. (If we go into Hereford we leave by
B4224, rejoining the route at Mordiford on the other side of
the river Lugg.)

On our way to Withington we cross A465 right-handed by the
'Cross Keys' inn, and in the village we go forward at the war
memorial cross, leaving the spired church on our left, then over a
crossroads for Bartestree. We cross the next major road left-
handed, then go straight on for two miles, crossing a second
major road, until we reach a T-junction, where we turn left over

the river. The views from this road to the wooded hills round Hereford are especially beautiful. Half a mile beyond the river we turn right at a major road T-junction then left on B4224, which we reach in under a mile and where we are rejoined by the Hereford sightseers. Immediately we turn left again on the minor road signposted Broadmoor, now driving right across the wooded hills and over Broadmoor Common to Woolhope where just beyond the church, an interesting one of Norman foundation, we turn left at the T-junction, then fork right for Putley.

We follow the signposts towards Putley, turning right at a T-junction, left in a quarter of a mile, and over a crossroads. Now we are on a high shelf road with grand views to the Malvern Hills, and as we descend we turn left at a T-junction for Poolend (leaving the road to Putley). This road takes us through extensive orchards and at Poolend joins A438, in which we turn right for half a mile, then left on A417 towards Leominster, leaving this straight Roman road in turn a mile beyond Ashperton for a turning on the right signposted Bishop's Frome. This pleasant little minor road follows the valley of the river Frome, taking us through the small village of Canon Frome to Castle Frome on B4214 (scarcely anything of the castle remains though the spired church is an interesting one dating from Norman times). To reach Bishop's Frome we turn left in B4214, crossing A4103 *en route*. Bishop's Frome lies among orchards and hop gardens. Its towered church also dates from the Norman period and has a good Norman south doorway with intricate moulding and a chancel arch in the same style.

After passing the church we leave the Bromyard road (B4214) for a turning on the right for Acton and Suckley. We follow the signposts to these two villages, crossing a major road at Acton Green, whence the signposts are a sure guide for the return to Worcester over quiet and fertile orchard and hop country, only joining the main road a mile or two from the city's outskirts.

The last route is a short tour for an afternoon for those living or staying in the Worcestershire border towns, such as Kidderminster, Stourport or Bewdley or, of course, from Worcester via A44 and A4025. It is routed from Stourport, reached by A451 from Kidderminster, and thence goes through Bewdley. We cross the Severn at Stourport (page 115) for Great Witley and

take the first turning on the right on the other side of the bridge,
signposted Ribbesford, and on reaching B4194 in just over half a
mile turn right for Bewdley. This is a lovely riverside road, the
wide Severn close beside us on our right and the wooded ridge
of Ribbesford Woods rising above us on our left.

After two and a half miles we reach the outskirts of Bewdley
(there is no sign of a village at Ribbesford, the spired church
in the park of Ribbesford House being the only reminder of the
former settlement). Bewdley is an ancient town which can boast
of a charter granted in 1472. Its fine bridge over the Severn is
on the site of one built in the Middle Ages, and near the river
there are some Tudor and Jacobean houses. The town itself,
however, has a Georgian aspect, with fine eighteenth-century
houses along the High Street, one of which has become the post
office, and its church was rebuilt in the classical style in 1746.
At the church we go forward on the Bridgnorth road (still
numbered B4194), turning right at the central junction. Our
road follows the bank of the Severn for almost a mile farther
then bears away from it into the heart of Wyre Forest, which
stretches out in all directions, a beautiful wooded vista wherever
we look.

This delightful road takes us right across Wyre Forest from
south-east to north-west, going through one little settlement in
a clearing; when we finally emerge from the woodlands, nearly
500 ft up, we have some splendid views over the Severn valley
to the right and to the Clee Hills and the other Shropshire hills
ahead. Where our road forks right for Bridgnorth we keep
straight on for Cleobury Mortimer, in just under a mile bearing
left where Cleobury is again signposted but in Bradley we leave
the Cleobury road, forking right on a minor road for Stottesdon.
This quiet road takes us through woodlands for the first mile
and beyond them we have a distant view to the right of Kinlet
Hall, an attractive early Georgian red brick house with stone
facings. The Norman church is adjacent to the manor-house.

We go forward at the junction by the 'Miners Arms', then
turn right a quarter of a mile beyond the inn and drive into
Stottesdon down a steep hill and up again, for Stottesdon stands
at about 600 ft. We turn left at the 'Cock' inn in this hilltop
village, leaving the church on our right. It is, however, worth
making a detour to see its beautiful Decorated work, its Saxon

doorway under the tower, and the Norman font ornamented with intricate designs.

We drive steeply downhill again, aiming towards the now imminent Brown Clee Hill, and at a T-junction turn right for Loughton, keeping left at the foot of the hill, again for Loughton, shortly crossing an open railway track and then the pretty river Rea. Now the way is straightforward to Loughton, two and a half miles distant from the river crossing. We pass on our left the tiny church beside a farm, one of the very few churches built during the reign of King James I, just before Loughton's crossroads, where we go forward for Burwarton, turning right at a major road T-junction in half a mile. We drive through Burwarton, with the park of the hall on the left and the village on the right of the road, and go straight on for Cleobury North, our road following the lower slopes of Brown Clee.

At Cleobury North we turn left at the crossroads for Ditton Priors, then left again uphill for Abdon and left at a triangular unsignposted junction. We turn right on the slopes of the hill and continue on this fine shelf road to Abdon, with splendid views as we encircle Brown Clee, reaching a height of well over 1,100 ft (the summit is only just under 1,800 ft). We descend gradually into Abdon when we leave this wonderful shelf road after about two miles, at a crossroads turning left for Clee St Margaret.

At Clee St Margaret we turn left through the village and left again for Stoke St Milborough, passing the church, which has some early Norman features, and some picturesque cottages. We soon reach Stoke St Milborough, the last of the string of pleasant villages round the foot of Brown Clee. It takes its name from St Milburga, to whom the church is dedicated and who founded Wenlock abbey (later it became a priory) in the seventh century. Nothing of the early church remains but there is some good early Gothic work in the later church built on the site, and nearby there is a well known as St Milburga's Well. At the T-junction beyond this ancient settlement we turn right for Ludlow, thence following this road to a major road, B4364, where we turn right again for Ludlow. We leave the Ludlow road, however, after a mile and a quarter, for a turning to Bitterley on the left, bearing right almost immediately for the latter. Bitterley is an ancient settlement under the western slopes of Titterstone

Clee Hill. It has a mainly late Norman church, with a number of interesting monuments inside, and a good churchyard cross outside, while there are a number of old houses in and around the village. Here we turn left where Clee Hill is signposted, and left again in a subsequent main road. This road takes us over a shoulder of Clee Hill with fine viewpoints to the right where we can pause and enjoy the extensive vistas.

After two and a half miles we turn right for Coreley, driving steeply downhill, and at Coreley go on for Milson. At Milson we turn right at the T-junction where Tenbury Wells is signposted, then bear left for Neen Sollars. Neen Sollars is a pretty village set between two rivers and almost surrounded by them, the Mill brook and the river Rea. We cross the Mill brook into the village and go forward through the village past its fourteenth-century spired church, crossing the river Rea at the other end of the village. We go through Neens Hill and in another mile reach a main road, A456, in which we turn left for Mamble and continue through this village on the main road to Clows Top. Here we turn right on the Worcester road at the crossroads by 'Ye Olde Crown' inn and follow this road for three miles as far as Abberley. We turn left into the village, passing the Victorian spired church which stands in the midst of fields, and bear left to the junction by the 'Manor Arms', opposite which is the ruined Norman church of St Michael, the original parish church and now partly restored. We bear right past the church, our road parallel with the wooded slopes of Abberley Hill and later we climb the lower slopes and after rounding the northerly nose of the hill shortly reach the main road, A451, in which we turn left for the return to Bewdley or Stourport, and thence to Kidderminster or right to join A443 near Great Witley for Worcester.

This final tour is perhaps an undramatic end to our exploration of the West Country, but the beautiful wooded hills, the sequestered villages on and under their slopes, and the picturesque riverside settlements we visit are typical of the quiet charm of the Marcher counties.

INDEX OF PLACES

Motoring on Regional Byways Series
by Christopher Trent

*To serve as companions and guides to places of natural
beauty and historic interest along unfrequented ways*

NORTH OF LONDON

Byway motoring within a 50-mile radius of the metropolis north
of the Thames.

LAKELAND

Byway motoring in Cumberland, Westmorland and the Furness
district of Lancashire.

MIDLAND ENGLAND

Byway motoring within a 50-mile radius of Birmingham and the
Black Country.

SOUTH OF LONDON

Byway motoring in Surrey, Kent and Sussex.

WEST COUNTRY

Byway motoring in Somerset, Gloucestershire, Herefordshire,
Shropshire, Worcestershire.

BORDER COUNTRY

Byway motoring in Northumberland, Durham and the border
country of Scotland.